W9-BFY-225

PRAISE FOR *YOUR CAREER ASSET*

"This is the clearest guidebook we have to one of the next frontiers of personal finance and financial planning: managing and monitoring the valuable career asset with the same care and diligence as you would tend an investment portfolio."

—**BOB VERES**, Inside Information and former
editor of *Financial Planning Magazine*

"This book helped me to think about my career, how I am managing this very important asset and how I might do even more to be intentional. I like the real world examples, featuring the career asset as primary with the key support of financial assets (and the necessary planning)."

—**DEBORAH L. FORD,** Chancellor,
University of Wisconsin-Parkside

"In this ground-breaking book, Mike Haubrich transforms how we each think about and manage our careers. Its appealing mix of theory, story, and actionable steps will make it the go-to classic resource for individuals rethinking career issues and for financial advisors who want to stay current with fundamental best practices."

—**PAULA HOGAN**, Financial Planning Advisor &
author of *Wealthinking* blog and *Trust Quarterly*

"Imagine treating your career as your most valuable workplace asset, and learning how to maximize it for greatest financial reward and life

satisfaction. Your Career Asset *clearly explains this brilliant framework, why it matters to you and to those whose careers you guide, and how to apply it, step-by-step. It will change how you think about your work and your career and more important, what to do about it."*

—EDWARD JACOBSON, PhD, MBA,
author of *Appreciative Moments: Stories and Practices for Living and Working Appreciatively*

"This book is a terrific inter-disciplinary resource. Mike Haubrich brings his innovative thinking, spirit of collaboration and passion for providing exceptional client service to life in the publication of this hands-on gem."

—JANE SCHROEDER, MS, Momentum Partners

CAREER
ASSET
MANAGEMENT

CAREER

ASSET

MANAGEMENT

*Getting Ahead, Staying Ahead and Using Your Head
to Maximize Your Career Value*

MICHAEL HAUBRICH, CFP®

WITH **TAMI WITT**

Advantage®

Published by Advantage, Charleston, South Carolina.
Member of Advantage Media Group.

ADVANTAGE is a registered trademark and the Advantage colophon is a trademark of Advantage Media Group, Inc.

Printed in the United States of America.

ISBN: 978-159932-509-5
LCCN: 2014941846

Book design by Megan Elger.

This publication is designed to provide accurate and authoritative information in regard to the subject matter covered. It is sold with the understanding that the publisher is not engaged in rendering legal, accounting, or other professional services. If legal advice or other expert assistance is required, the services of a competent professional person should be sought.

This publication includes discussions, examples, and representations to provide authoritative information in regard to the topic. Information derived from other sources is presumed to be accurate but is not guaranteed by the author or publisher. Ideas and advice offered in this book are intended to be suggestions and may not be suitable for your situation. The author shall not be liable for any loss of income or any other damages. Names used in examples and stories have been changed to protect privacy.

Advantage Media Group is proud to be a part of the Tree Neutral® program. Tree Neutral offsets the number of trees consumed in the production and printing of this book by taking proactive steps such as planting trees in direct proportion to the number of trees used to print books. To learn more about Tree Neutral, please visit **www.treeneutral.com**. To learn more about Advantage's commitment to being a responsible steward of the environment, please visit **www.advantagefamily.com/green**

Advantage Media Group is a publisher of business, self-improvement, and professional development books and online learning. We help entrepreneurs, business leaders, and professionals share their Stories, Passion, and Knowledge to help others Learn & Grow. Do you have a manuscript or book idea that you would like us to consider for publishing? Please visit **advantagefamily.com** or call **1.866.775.1696**.

To my grandmother, who exemplified
the power of the human spirit
and taught me the value of perseverance.

ACKNOWLEDGMENTS

I have many people to thank for helping bring this book into being. There is always the risk of missing someone, so I'll apologize in advance, and to those below, I couldn't have done this without you.

First, last and always, Tami Witt, my writer, champion, best friend, and partner in all ways.

Bob Veres, thanks for your encouragement, exposure, and for being an early advocate of the concept and providing a platform to introduce CAM to the financial planning industry.

Pam Kassner, my public relations consultant, who worked with the media in getting the first CAM Makeovers profiled and managed public relations as we developed the model.

My business partner, Justus Morgan, CFP®, for being my steady sounding board and for keeping the wheels—and our team—on the bus while I was researching and developing the CAMs model for clients and our industry.

The rest of my Financial Services Group team, including Terri Larson, Justin Moilanen, Kim Molbeck, Bob Francour, and Lori Jozefiak, whose eye for detail helped make sure we got this done.

My editor, Pat Speer, who had the best timing in bringing her unique talents to help get the book ready for print.

Others to whom I owe many thanks include Pauline Foster, Paula Hogan, Janine Moon, Jane Schroeder, Robert Schumann, Cali Yost, Mary Jo King, Steve Biel, my many friends and colleagues in the financial planning industry, and, of course, my clients.

Thank you all for your encouragement, patience, and the many big and little things you did to bring this book to life for our readers.

And finally, but certainly not least, to anyone who reads this book and perhaps comes away with an idea or two that can be applied in building, managing, and optimizing your career asset. We wish you all the best!

CONTENTS

INTRODUCTION

When we think of financial asset classes a few come immediately to mind. Cash, stocks, bonds, insurance and other investments such as real estate—in other words, the things you own that allow you to buy and build new assets, pay off debts and enable you to afford the lifestyle that aligns with your goals and values.

The premise of this book is that your career can and should be viewed as an asset on par with all those others. In fact, it's fair to say that without a sustainable career asset, accumulating other assets would be a whole lot harder, if not downright impossible, to do.

Assets are built upon over time, can be optimized and leveraged as appropriate for different life phases, and need to be properly managed in order to ensure sustainability.

Without a sustainable career asset, accumulating other assets would be a whole lot harder, if not downright impossible, to do.

This book outlines how to think of your career the same way: How to develop, manage, and optimize your work to create and sustain a thriving asset that fortifies the other assets in your portfolio. A career, like other assets, advances over time and through a series of strategies, enabling you to enter and remain in a field of work. Your career development includes work experiences, education, training, and other things that contribute to increasing your knowledge, skills, and talents, thereby increasing your marketplace value.

Managing your career involves enhancing skills, navigating workplace politics, networking within your industry or profession, timing conversations with your boss or supervisor, knowing how to balance self-promotion/marketing, knowing when to leave a role or take a new assignment, anticipating what the future holds—not easy tasks by any measure. Optimizing your career involves ensuring that it is working for you and helping you achieve the overall well-being you desire while contributing to whatever definition of success you hold for yourself.

However, the task of developing, managing and optimizing your career is not a linear process that follows prescribed steps. Rather, your career is fluid, dynamic, and subject to planned or unplanned changes. The disclaimer "past performance is not an indication of future returns" applies to a career as it does to investments. Just because something led to success in the past, doesn't mean continuing the same thing will result in the same or better outcomes. Therefore, agility and flexibility are critical in accomplishing your career asset goals.

In this book, you'll discover how career volatility and velocity can impact your career asset and how to calculate your total career value using quantitative and qualitative factors. You'll learn how much money you'll need to have in reserve to fund career transitions of various types. You'll benefit from the examples of others who demonstrate what it means to own your career and how they have taken steps to gain or regain work+life fit that helps ensure a longer active career life. We'll share insights about three essential habits that enhance your career value. You'll see how the six-step process used by financial planners can be applied to your career asset and the impact different career phases have on your career asset. We'll explain the differences among the various resources who can partner with you in developing, managing and optimizing your career asset.

A LONG AND WINDING ROAD

You may be wondering how a veteran financial planner developed such a committed passion to the topic of career optimization. Well, let me explain how my journey began and where it has led me so far, recognizing, of course, that I'm still en route in my own learning and discovering.

More than 35 years ago, I began my career in the financial services industry as an insurance agent with a large, nationally recognized insurance company. At the time, I was motivated by the simple basic needs a young father of one—with my second on the way— typically experiences. I needed to provide for my family. Fortunately, I had a good mind for numbers and a deeply instilled work ethic that I learned from my grandmother, who raised me following the death of my mother when I was five years old.

A German immigrant with minimal education, my grandmother worked tirelessly to set an example and shape my moral character. Self-taught, she was a savvy businesswoman who owned and operated three community-based residential care facilities for veterans suffering from post-traumatic stress disorder and other forms of mental illness or disability.

From the time I was 12 years old, I helped her cook and clean and manage the facilities that served as home to more than 20 veterans. I learned early the value of a hard day's work, of contributing to something bigger than myself, of adding value where and when I could to help ease the burden and bring a little peace of mind to those we served.

Under my grandmother's watchful guidance, I learned how to negotiate with vendors (and residents), how to manage accounts, and how to plan ahead. Besides being an excellent role model for teaching practical life skills, my grandmother taught me how to think for myself and march to my own drummer. It was during these formative years that I discovered I was good at selling—ideas or items, it didn't matter—I was good at it. I learned how to listen, not only to what people were saying, but to what they weren't saying out loud. I became a watchful observer of human behavior. I learned how people react and respond, particularly in stressful situations, and how emotions can hijack the decision-making process. Over time, I learned how discipline and logic could be used as tools to help others avoid making life-altering and potentially damaging decisions, particularly when it came to their personal finances.

When I started my career in the insurance business at the insurance company, I should have expected how it would turn out. In retrospect, I should have known I would likely not be one to achieve my personal definition of success while working for someone else. I had spent too much of my life under the tutelage of an entrepreneur and self-made woman. I was used to and comfortable with making my own decisions and choices about priorities, process, and profitability. Having someone else try and dictate those things to me felt downright unnatural.

While successful in my role selling insurance, it wasn't long before I discovered what for me presented a true conflict of interest. In my first nine months I was on pace to be rookie salesman of the year for the region. Regardless of that early accomplishment, I was informed my pay was going to be reduced because I was not selling the "right kind" of insurance. If I wanted to maximize my income, I was told I needed to sell expensive cash value insurance to the children of parents I was working with, not just the low-cost term insurance for the household breadwinner. Recognizing the low-cost term insurance was exactly what was needed to help ensure the security for those families, I had to make a choice—do what I believed was in the best interest of my clients or what my employer who paid me wanted and expected of me. I chose the best interest of my clients.

Not surprisingly, within a couple of months I was fired. However, the positive outcome of that experience was the realization that my commitment to reducing or eliminating conflicts of interest would increase my ability to provide the highest value—even if it meant I collected a little less pay. I realized the only way I could honor this commitment was to be self-employed or establish my own company where I set the rules for how we would interact with clients. Even before I cognitively viewed my career as an asset, I knew I wasn't maximizing its value and wanted (and, in fact, needed) to do something different in order to bring my values and my career into better alignment.

Even before I cognitively viewed my career as an asset, I knew I wasn't maximizing its value.

Borrowing from the idiom "necessity is the mother of invention," I built Financial Service Group to help meet the financial planning needs of others in order for them to have the life they dream of having.

Today, Financial Service Group is a fee-only financial planning firm inspiring the financial well-being of clients across America. Being true to the commitment to reduce or eliminate potential conflicts of interest, we don't sell financial products for commission. We are motivated to help our clients achieve their financial and life goals though well-conceived and executed financial life planning. Perhaps replicating the safe environment I once watched my grandmother create for the veterans, Financial Service Group provides a safe and comfortable atmosphere to share even the most intimate ideas, goals, aspirations, fears, concerns, tragedies, and celebrations. Our firm is proud of our commitment to our values of integrity, compassion and excellence.

THE BIRTH OF AN IDEA

It was about 2004 when I first began seeing a greater number of my later-career stage clients coming in to discuss the idea of early retirement. Retirement planning is one of the primary catalysts for seeking the counsel of a financial advisor and certainly a core of our business offering. While the ideas of accelerating the timeline to retirement were not new, the frequency of these conversations and their emotional intensity seemed to be pointing to an emerging trend.

Over time I began noticing that clients were actually looking for an alternative to dissatisfying, unfulfilling work and the most obvious alternative was NOT working at all. At that time, the economy was strong and we were enjoying record-high stock returns. Clients were seeing their well-funded 401Ks and other retirement savings growing and yielding higher-than-average returns. Why not use that asset to fund early retirement?

What these clients didn't recognize was that their desire to retire early was only one strategy for dealing with a dysfunctional career that no longer satisfied their emotional, intellectual, social, or perhaps even their financial, objectives. In the throes of emotional discomfort, the conclusion of not working seemed better than going to work every day and being miserable.

Collaborating with career coaches and counselors, I began doing extensive research into career dynamics, career life spans, and life stages. I became a student of thought-leaders and authors such as Donald Super, Daniel Pink, Marc Freedman, Marshall Goldsmith, Cali Yost, and Tom Rath to better understand what motivates and drives people in their careers. I began to better understand how theories and levers popularized in employee engagement studies contributed to employee retention. I wanted to better understand work-place flexibility and the many alternatives to what we consider a traditional work life that were available. In other words, I dove into a lot of what would be considered human resource-related topics and even attended human capital conferences to learn more about workforce demographics and emerging trends in employee attitudes, beliefs, work structures, motivators, and engagement. I wanted to know how employers were responding to the growing wave of want-to-be retirees and what they were doing (or were willing to do) to retain late career stage talent.

What these clients didn't recognize was that their desire to retire early was only one strategy for dealing with a dysfunctional career that no longer satisfied their emotional, intellectual, social, or perhaps even their financial, objectives.

To truly understand where my clients were coming from, I felt it was important to understand the environments in which they worked every day. From there, I felt I needed to explore what companies were planning or actively doing to address an aging population of talent that was increasingly at risk of disengaging from long-term employers because of dissatisfaction, disinterest, or disengagement.

This trifecta of dissatisfaction-disinterest-disengagement became the catalyst for what I considered a logical marriage of traditional financial planning and career asset planning. As a result, Career Asset Management was born and integrated into Financial Service Group's service delivery model.

I felt so strongly that the career asset was not being given the attention it deserved by the financial planning industry that I spent more than a year introducing the idea of Career Asset Management to other financial planners through national conferences and seminars. My goal was to have "career" adopted as an asset class along with the more traditional standbys of stocks, bonds, cash, real estate, and alternative investments.

I felt there was a place in the financial planning process to integrate the value of a person's career. Unlike some of the other asset classes, a career asset is, perhaps, the most important asset a person will hold, because ultimately, its value, performance and sustainability are under the person's complete and total control.

Unlike some of the other asset classes, a career asset is, perhaps, the most important asset a person will hold, because ultimately, its value, performance and sustainability are under the person's complete and total control.

We started hearing more and more industry buzz about career as an asset. Financial planners began adopting strategies that intentionally and proactively addressed career in their financial planning conversations with clients. Today, it's not at all uncommon to find financial planners and career coaches/counselors sharing office space or otherwise closely collaborating. Career continues to gain industry acceptance as an asset class and more financial planners are adopting Career Asset Management into their service delivery models.

SO HOW DOES CAREER ASSET MANAGEMENT REALLY WORK?

Consider an employee with peak wages of $75,000 who abruptly retires at age 60. Now let's consider what it would look like if that person's career were extended for an additional eight years. During the first three years the employee works at 75 percent of current schedule and income, the next three years they work/earn at 60 percent, and work/earn at 40 percent for the last two years. Assuming an average income and employment tax rate of 40 percent and a 6-percent discount rate, the value in today's dollar of that increased income is $174,150. By any standard, that's a good return on investment.

We're oversimplifying here by only considering income. In this book, you'll see how other quantifiable measures of a career asset, such as employee benefits, increased pension, and Social Security benefit accruals, contribute to career asset value. Plus, there are qualitative (non-financial) factors, such as job satisfaction and social interaction that are also taken into consideration. You'll see how developing, managing and optimizing your career asset impacts your long-term financial well-being, and you'll discover an easy-to-recall analogy that will help you continue to view your career as something you own and can allow others to benefit from for a period of time.

By studying this issue for more than a decade, collaborating with career development professionals, and working with many clients, we have learned that by reframing career as a financial asset, we can objectively advise and facilitate action-oriented discussions and changes. By reviewing the data with clients, we can help them get past emotions that have the potential of hijacking effective decision-making and rational action related to their career asset.

This book offers a few new perspectives about career as it relates to financial and overall life well-being. While you're reading, you may experience a paradigm shift in the way you view the spectrum of options between full employment and not working at all. This shift in thinking enables you to extend and evolve your career asset so it continues to fuel your financial engine longer than you may believe possible.

YOUR MOST VALUABLE ASSET

A 2012 *PARADE* magazine and a Yahoo! Finance job satisfaction/ happiness survey of 26,000 Americans revealed that 60 percent of the respondents would choose a different career if given the chance. So what keeps that majority from making a change?

The most likely answer is fear—fear of starting over, fear of losing a comfortable, well-earned salary, fear of failing at something new or not recognizing what truly inspires them. In fact, career counselors report that employees' fear associated with financial factors is the most significant roadblock to making changes that could improve their work+life fit and career circumstances.

During the last decade, an increasing number of financial advisors began incorporating conversations about a client's career with their investments, homes, retirement accounts, and other traditional assets. Adjusting the paradigm to view career as an asset involves adjusting behaviors to focus on developing, managing and optimizing that asset with the objective of increasing its value.

CAREER ASSET DEFINED

Let's start with one definition of "career asset" from vocational psychologist Donald Super. Super suggests your career asset is the value-for-value exchange of your time, talent, and potential in the three dimensions of employment, family, and community spread over your lifetime.

In this book we will focus primarily on what Super describes as the dimension of employment; however, the impact of family and community extends the career asset throughout the entire lifecycle. We can and should continue to exchange our time, talent and potential outside of the dimension of employment with fulfilling activities such as volunteer work in our communities, and by being a fully committed and engaged member of family and societal relationships. Under this broad definition, our career asset has value throughout our lifetime—and it shifts continuously among the dimensions of employment, family, and community with each dimension impacting the other dimensions.

Because of its influence on other dimensions of life, you should manage your career asset to maximize its long-term return just as you would manage other assets. Your career asset return on investment is made up of not only the current salary you are paid, but the satisfaction you receive by doing what really energizes and engages you. That is much harder to quantify but no less an important consideration in managing your career asset. Failing to balance work and life objectives increases your risk of suffering career burnout, which manifests in reduced productivity, stress-related health issues, and fewer number of work years before retirement. All of these factors have a corresponding impact on your financial sustainability.

Your career asset return on investment is made up of not only the current salary you are paid, but the satisfaction you receive by doing what really energizes and engages you.

For those people who may be dissatisfied with their job or career for myriad and often very legitimate reasons, retirement comes to be viewed as an escape from a dysfunctional work environment that no longer fits their work and life objectives. They're unhappy and believe there is a black or white solution and that is to either retire or simply quit. Either of these choices have significant financial impacts.

If you opt to retire early and start collecting benefits, you may reduce your financial or other benefits; if you just flat out quit, you're also quitting on your employer-funded benefits, potentially walking out on unexercised stock options, to say nothing of cutting off an income stream that you've doubtlessly grown accustomed to having in order to support your financial, family, and other life goals.

In viewing career as a financial asset that can be developed, managed, and optimized, a range of flexible alternatives—on the continuum between quitting and not working at all to working full time until retirement—become available for consideration.

Along that continuum are flexible options such as reduced- or part-time work, consulting, freelancing, contract project engagements, limited engagement assignments, job sharing, flexible work scheduling, identified term contracts and other options that may offer a more satisfying work+life fit. Any of these options may result in higher levels of job satisfaction, which, in turn, lead to career longevity thereby enhancing and preserving your career asset.

THE IMPORTANCE OF WORK+LIFE FIT

Many companies today are escalating the conversation about work+life fit as they come to recognize its impact on employee engagement, productivity, and retention. They are becoming increasingly open to and creative in their approaches related to programs and policies aimed at fitting employees' work lives into the rest of their lives rather than the other way around. But the burden for achieving optimal work+life fit that serves the needs of both the employee and the employer is not the sole responsibility of the employer. Employees, as the owners of their career asset, must also take responsibility for their work+life fit.

Employees, as the owners of their career asset, must also take responsibility for their work+life fit.

By taking steps to ensure your work and other aspects of your life are optimally fit for you, you're helping to manage your career asset in a way that will maximize your investment in your time, talent, and potential. Managing that balance will also help ensure that you remain in the work force longer than if this delicate balance is not maintained.

So how do you manage your work and life balance to protect your career asset? In her book, *Work + Life Finding a Fit That's Right for You*, Cali Williams Yost details a three-step process designed to activate you toward optimum balance. The process she advocates involves a combination of introspection, planning, and action.

Step one serves to challenge the way we think about work and life and dispel some of the common misconceptions we hold as fact. She presents eight fundamentals to help create a work-life fit that enables long-term satisfaction and sustainability. Her eight fundamentals are:

- *Taking the initiative – doing the work to create and propose a better work+life fit*

- *Seeing the possibilities – there are an infinite number of possibilities between 100 percent work and not working at all*

- *Asking and getting to yes – believing that what you propose will be accepted rather than assuming it will be rejected*

- *Believing you add value – Knowing the value you bring to your company/role*

- *Making the business case – demonstrating what's in it for your company as well as what's in it for you*

- *Knowing that your reason is a good reason – regardless of the reason for your work+life fit proposal, it is valid and it meets the needs of the business*

- *Being flexible – my work+life vision might evolve over time, so what I propose today may not be the permanent state*

- *Being patient and persistent – taking the time to think through your optimal work+life fit, and developing a proposal that identifies what's in it for your employers, knowing that it might take a while to work the process - (Yost, 2004)*

Each of the fundamentals is backed by case histories and anecdotal stories designed to encourage and motivate you to achieve the best fit for your personal situation. Yost presents compelling questions that challenge you to take a thoughtful, measured approach to identifying your work+life fit needs and expectations.

An advocate of Career Asset Management, Yost also includes exercises designed to stretch your thinking about your career as an asset that you develop, manage, and optimize through effective work+life fit strategies.

In the next step, Yost suggests you identify real or perceived road-blocks that can derail you from achieving productive balance. Fear of success or of failure, resistance to change, and in-the-box thinking are factors that have the potential to prevent an individual from effectively developing, managing and optimizing their career asset. In "Work+Life," Yost shares stories of others who have dealt with these challenges and offers suggestions for how to overcome them.

After doing the self-work in the first two steps, step three centers on creating an actual roadmap and business case to help you develop, manage, and optimize your career as an asset that provides the work+life fit that contributes to your career longevity and sustainability.

How does achieving work+life fit relate to the financial planning process?

The more traditional financial planning process tends to view a person's career as more or less static and takes a binary approach—typical financial planning clients either work *or* retire. That traditional model does not allow for the flexible options mentioned earlier in this chapter.

Let's look at two different approaches.

John seeks the counsel of a financial planner because he wants to retire in the near-term future at age 60. He finds his job stressful and feels he has a serious work+life imbalance.

Following the traditional model, the financial planner focuses on retirement projection and portfolio issues based on John retiring at age 60. Ultimately John retires and is successful in reducing his job-related stress. Unfortunately, after a few years and despite getting what he said he wanted, John is still fundamentally unhappy. He is feeling unfulfilled, concerned about running out of money, and socially out of place with his still-working circle of friends. He misses his work relationships, feelings of adding value, and the intellectual stimulation of contributing to solving problems. He simply misses being in the game. He got out of a stressful job, but that move created different stressors for John. The black-or-white solution of work versus retire solves one problem, but presents him with a whole list of new ones.

John's friend Jane has the same issue. Her work no longer generates any passion or excitement. At age 59 she doesn't want to continue working at a job that doesn't satisfy her and views retirement as a logical alternative. Jane seeks the counsel of a different financial planner who gathers information on Jane's financial position and goals, and then validates Jane's concerns about stress and job satisfaction. The planning conversation then progresses to a discussion about potential alternatives to retirement that may extend the useful life of Jane's career and allow her to continue to grow her financial assets while achieving an improved work situation.

Let's assume at the time of the initial visit John and Jane both had peak wages of $150,000. Working through an intentional approach, Jane's planner is able to help her consider and negotiate a more fulfilling employment arrangement. For three years she will work 75 percent of her former hours and earn 75 percent of her peak income; the next three years she'll work 60 percent of her former hours and earn 60 percent of her peak income. Then she'll work for two more years at 40 percent of her hours and peak income.

Under this plan, Jane will work for eight additional years, retire gradually and enjoy increasing amounts of free time that she can use in other more satisfying pursuits. After subtracting an average income and employment tax rate of 40 percent and assuming a 6 percent discount rate, the net present value of those eight years of additional income as a result of Jane's decision to alter her work but remain employed is $348,300. Let's say Jane's investment portfolio at the time of her initial visit was $1 million. Her decision to remain employed, following a gradual reduced work schedule with reduced wages would result in an increase in her net worth of more than 33 percent.

And this isn't even a complete accounting!

The value of extending Jane's career by eight years also includes employee benefits, pension and Social Security accruals. The numbers also don't account for intangibles, such as the ability to maintain the social interaction, status and self-actualization benefits experienced from and through meaningful work.

John may have accomplished his goal of retiring as an exit strategy for a less-than-desirable work situation, but Jane renegotiated her deal so she could achieve the work+life fit she wanted while she continued to increase her career asset.

IS YOUR CAREER A TRIPLE NET LEASE IN DISGUISE?

You may be familiar with the concept of triple net lease commonly used in commercial and retail sales real estate. Under a triple net lease the landlord establishes a long-term contract with a tenant, sometimes as long as ten, 20 or even 30 years. Under the terms of that long-term lease, the tenant behaves like they own the property, assuming responsibility for paying the taxes, making improvements, arranging the maintenance, and optimizing the property. The landlord collects rents but real "ownership" responsibilities fall to the long-term tenant.

If you think about it, this was the work philosophy that was common 30, 40, or 50 years ago. Employees sought a workplace that could become their employment home. It was common for employees to work for a single employer for their entire career with many clocking in 40 years or more in service to the same company, effectively leasing their career to the employer for the long-term. In those days, there was often a mutual understanding that an employee would remain loyal to an employer who, in exchange for that loyalty, would "take care of" the employee and be responsible for developing and managing their career to the extent the employer wanted the employee to grow and advance. The employee's main responsibility was to be loyal, show up on time, be productive, and not make waves. As long as they did those things and performed the primary job duties, the lease of their career would continue.

But the wheels of progress slow for no one, and as product and service lifecycles collapsed, product relevancy to consumers shortened, and the economy shifted from an industrial base to a knowledge base, changes in employment durations also changed. That once-held implied contract for loyal service in exchange for long-term employment was irrevocably broken. Employee attitudes around being taken care of also shifted to ones around taking care of themselves. Employees came to recognize (often with employers reinforcing the notion) that each employee "owns" their career and they, not the employer, are ultimately responsible for developing, managing and optimizing it. This lets the employer off the hook for developing employees and shifts the burden for continuous self-improvement to the owner of the asset—the employee.

The average worker today changes jobs a minimum of nine times and it's reasonable to expect to change careers at least three times during a working lifetime.

By and large, Generation Y employees (those 71 million people born between 1977 and 1994) are not interested in long-term commitments with employers. The growing attention to being able to achieve work+life balance through flexible work options will certainly be no less significant for the 23 million Generation Z employees who come of age between 2013 and 2020.

Additionally, employers need to have a more flexible, agile workforce to allow them to remain financially competitive and responsive to market trends and customer demands. Off-shoring, out-sourcing, top-sizing and forced ranking are just some of the strategies that influence workforce planning and management.

Triple net leases of an employee's career asset do not represent a value proposition for the employee or the employer. According to the U.S. Department of Labor, the average worker today changes jobs a minimum of nine times and it's reasonable to expect to change careers at least three times during a working lifetime.

THE LANDLORD OF YOUR CAREER

Let's continue to build on this idea of your career as something you own but that you rent out to others to use for a specified timeframe. We'll use a piece of rental property to illustrate this idea.

In the case of a rental property, the property owner is highly motivated to secure a responsible tenant. The property owner knows he/she needs to offer a good value proposition to attract a quality, responsible, and potentially long-term tenant. In order to attract the best renters who are willing to pay market-value rent, the property has to be in good shape, present well, and offer features and amenities that are valued by today's standards. For example, there was a time when finding a rental unit that had a dishwasher would be considered a higher-end or luxury unit. Today, a dishwasher is a must-have for professional, socially active tenants who leave little time in their hectic schedules for low value tasks such as hand-washing dishes.

An experienced property owner knows the worst tenants tend to be the ones who are willing to pay more than market rent. These often desperate tenants are the ones who are more likely to damage the rental unit since they're paying more for it than it's worth, so they feel justified in mistreating the property. A landlord knows it's far better to receive a fair rent from an ideal tenant rather than risk the sustainability of the asset by getting more than fair market price from a less than ideal tenant.

As the owner of your own career property, you recognize that you have to offer a good value proposition to employers and you work hard to build your skills, talents, and capabilities to make them attractive in the competitive job market. You ensure you're current with your industry's trends, you attend workshops and seminars to enhance your skills, and you look for special projects or short-term assignments that give you additional exposure and visibility. You fill your rental career asset with features and amenities that make you the most attractive value proposition for your tenant employer.

There may have been a time in your career where you rented your work to an abusive, disregarding, unreasonable tenant employer in exchange for some over-market pay. You were raking in some extra pay, but you paid a hefty price in terms of the work+life fit, stress management, job satisfaction, overall well-being and perhaps even career longevity. You know when that happens because you can *feel* the damage and you cognitively and emotionally recognize it's not a sustainable way to develop, manage, and optimize your career, even if you're unable or unwilling to make a change at the time.

KEEPING YOUR ASSET IN A RENT-READY STATE

Sometimes, just as in the case of a bad tenant, the landlord has to decide the cost is not worth the real or perceived benefit of continuing the relationship. The landlord gives appropriate notice to the tenant and the agreement ends.

As the landlord of your career, if deferred maintenance (career skill set) along with a destructive tenant (employer or negative work+life fit) are allowed to continue, over time the property's (your career) value will decline, the ability to increase rents (optimize talents, skills and experience) will be reduced, and the useful life of the property will diminish. The value of this mismanaged asset is minimized.

Evicting the destructive tenant (adjusting the negative work+life fit factors) and rehabbing the property (learning/applying new skills or changing jobs) results in increased future cash flow potential and extends the useful life of the property (career asset continuation).

In order to remain competitive and marketable to the world of tenant employers, employees need to keep up their "property," which comprises their talents, skills and experience, relevant to ever-changing economy and market demands.

In order to remain competitive and marketable to the world of tenant employers, employees need to keep up their "property," which comprises their talents, skills and experience, relevant to ever-changing economy and market demands.

Additionally, you also have to become acutely aware of your career value to the marketplace. You have to know what the work you do is worth to those you do it for.

Remember the days when the business world could barely survive without a stenographer? Those rapidly moving hands could capture 120 spoken words in a few swipes of a pen stroke then effortlessly transcribe them in triplicate using carbon paper and a manual typewriter. The lost art of shorthand may still be practiced by a few, but it's not a skill set I would want as the headliner on my résumé. It simply isn't valued in today's efficient, technology-enhanced workplace and it's not something that employers would necessarily pay extra to have. The same goes for switchboard and data-punch operators. According to the Bureau of Labor Statistics, by 2018 we'll see dramatic declines in employment for first-line manufacturing supervisors and machinists, as well as computer operators, desktop publishers, mail sorters and even semiconductor processors.

Being able to fairly and accurately assess how much the work you actually do is worth in relation to the worth of work that is actually needed is essential in estimating your career value. Market reference benchmarking is a way to assess that value and we'll get more into that in an upcoming chapter.

CAREER ASSET MAKEOVERS

The more clients I encountered who came to me interested in retiring as a black-or-white alternative to working, the more I considered the advantages of helping these clients discover new aspects of their career they might not have previously contemplated.

The desire to gain an improved or different work+life fit doesn't have to be result of career dissatisfaction at all. You may have a perfectly wonderful job, working with perfectly wonderful people, making a perfectly acceptable wage, but still be dissatisfied with your employment. You may be thinking that retirement must be the only option since you have a seemingly perfect gig and you're not happy, so there couldn't be anything—short of retiring—that *could* make you happy. However, life events such as the death of a spouse or other family member, empty nesting, inherited money, or threat of career obsolescence lead you to start questioning your career satisfaction and decisions about the type of work you do, where you do it and how you do it.

Life events are often just as significant as catalysts for change as is job dissatisfaction. In fact, life events or life transitions are the leading reason people seek the counsel of a financial advisor.

As a financial planner by trade, I knew that career coaching, counseling, and any form of psychological therapy were beyond my direct scope and it would be wise to collaborate with professionals from other areas to help my clients engage in

Life events are often just as significant as catalysts for change as is job dissatisfaction.

what I call "career makeovers." These makeovers presented the opportunity for self-exploration and strengths discovery as well as for a refreshed, rejuvenated career that could extend the life of the career asset and positively impact the individual's financial and overall well-being.

The idea of the career makeover was simple. Take a client in the throes of change as the result of a life event or career dissatisfaction and create a team of appropriate resources to help the client navigate the discovery process and explore alternative options with the intent of extending the career asset's value.

In this team approach, financial planners are engaged to fully understand the client's current financial position and goals and the impact of career changes on their personal financial landscape. A therapist might be included to address any financial dysfunction or harmful behaviors stemming from money scripts—many of which are formed in early childhood and continue to influence our choices, decisions, and actions around money throughout our lives. A career coach might work with the client on assessments and inventories to help identify talents and strengths that may be underused or not maximized. A résumé writer might be engaged to help the client repackage and reposition their work history.

In his book, *StrengthsFinder 2.0*, Tom Rath dispels the misguided maxim "You can be anything you want to be, if you just try hard enough." Rath argues that people develop talents at an early age that become instinctive and distinctive strengths when properly nourished. He goes on to propose that people do their best work when given the opportunity to use their strengths every day. Supporting his findings is extensive research by the Gallup Organization based on assessments of more than 10 million people.

According to Rath, "when we're able to put most of our energy into developing our natural talents, extraordinary room for growth exists." This alters the "you can be anything" maxim to align with Rath's conclusion, "you cannot be anything you want to be—but you can be a lot more of who you really are." (Rath, 2007)

Career makeovers gained traction and one client's journey was chronicled in a three-part series published in the Milwaukee Journal Sentinel in spring, 2006. In this case, the client was a 52-year-old single mother whose own mother recently died. Having inherited some money from her mother, she recognized that she now had a financial cushion to afford her the opportunity to re-evaluate her career and perhaps make some changes that would allow her to extend her career asset. At the time, she was a self-employed consultant who yearned for greater career fulfillment. She often found herself working with organizations on change but then never getting to see her recommended changes implemented. She wanted to be able to experience the whole process and she was tired of not having a work home to call her own.

In this career makeover, we put together a team to help her identify the ideal path that would lead her to increased satisfaction, using her skills and talents in a new career that would allow her to extend the value of her vital asset. Working with her on assessments and inventories, a career coach was able to help her identify strategies and options for entering a new career field that still used the strengths and skills she developed in her consulting practice but provided her with more of what she felt was lacking in that vocational path. As the financial advising resource on the team, I worked with her to help her manage her finances and fund her employment search, which took considerable time and financial resources. Together we identified how much she would need to earn to reach financial goals that would fund her current needs and her future retirement. This projection, as well as market research into the value of the type of work she wanted to do, provided the starting point for identifying and negotiating an equitable salary.

This career makeover had a happy ending. The client, after rejecting several job offers because they didn't fit her re-envisioned view of herself, landed what she describes as her ideal career. Now happily employed in a traditional job setting as a community relations director, she is experiencing higher levels of job satisfaction, financial security, and work+life fit than at any time in her career. Retirement isn't even under consideration at this time. Thoughts of retirement have been replaced with energy and passion for continuing her career. The value of her career asset continues to build every day which, in turn, will more effectively fund her eventual retirement in whatever form and shape that has at the time she's truly ready to retire.

OWNING YOUR CAREER

In developing Career Asset Management services I have had the good fortune of meeting with experts from around the country to share ideas and collaborate on the emerging perspective of career as an asset class. One of the career coaches I worked with is Janine Moon, a 30-plus-year veteran of mentoring, developing, and coaching others.

I first met Janine while researching career coaches in Ohio on behalf of a Certified Financial Planner® professional colleague who attended one of my conference presentations in 2006.

At the time, my colleague wanted to explore adding Career Asset Management to his financial life planning practice and was willing to facilitate a career makeover as a learning/exploration case study. The first thing we needed to do was find a good career coach/partner who would collaborate with him. Janine was willing to donate her time to meet with the subject of the makeover. I served as a consultant/mentor to the process, including performing the financial planning interviews alongside of the other planner. The career makeover was a success, resulting in the subject becoming clear about how she needed to optimize her career and negotiate a work+life fit she felt was more suitable.

Following this makeover, Janine and I continued to collaborate and ideate on further refinements of Career Asset Management. Janine was working on her book, *Career Ownership, Creating 'Job Security' in Any Economy*, which was published in 2010. Upon publishing the book, she presented her concepts at the Financial Planning Association's Annual Retreat.

Janine's book is one of our recommended readings for any client in a career transition. I also recommend the book to any young adult starting their first job or graduating from higher education. What I find most valuable in "Career Ownership" is the basic premise that as owners of our careers, we have the responsibility to act like owners. Janine offers ten questions designed to test if you really do own your career. I find these questions valuable in working with clients to help them assess the current state regarding how much (or how little) of their careers they really own.

> **As owners of our careers, we have the responsibility to act like owners.**

Do you own your career? Are you acting like an owner? Janine proposes the following questions will help you be able to tell:

- *When did you last consider your career "location?" Does it provide maximum satisfaction and the promise of enduring value for the investment you've made in your work life?*

- *When did you last conduct serious research to educate yourself about the future of your industry and the skills needed to succeed in this changing marketplace?*

- *When did you last assess your skills, abilities and goals to determine how you could gain the most satisfaction from the workspace in which you spend many of your waking hours?*

- *When did you last write out (of your own volition) your 3-year career plan along with your 12-month learning plan…and follow them?*

- *When did you last devote personal time and funds to upgrade your own skills?*

- *When did you last consider requesting a job rotation that would help you build relationships and impact your marketability inside or outside of your organization?*

- *When did you last talk to your manager about the additional value you provide to your clients and how you accomplish this?*

- *When did you last review and align yourself with your organization's top two strategic growth areas?*

- *When did you last identify any weak areas in your skills or performance and take personal responsibility to address the problem?*

- *When did you last have a conversation about how your work-life circumstances impact the important others in your life?* (Moon, 2010)

Taking time to be intentional in answering these questions and addressing the steps necessary to correct any identified deficiencies can be time-consuming, expensive and often inconvenient—but that's exactly what career owners do.

DETERMINING YOUR
TOTAL CAREER VALUE

Perhaps the single greatest mistake a person can make relative to career, is under- or over-estimating its true value. So what exactly is the "value" of a persons' career? First, it is essential to understand the various inputs that are used in completing a career valuation.

It seems reasonable that a person earning a salary that averages $150,000 per year places the value of their career at $150,000 times the number of years he or she is likely to earn at that level. To provide a simple example, let's use round numbers. You may estimate that you'll spend ten years of your career earning $75,000/year for a total of $750,000; another ten years earning $100,000 for a total of $1 million; and another ten years earning $150,000 for a total of $1.5 million, bringing your career projected wages total to roughly $2.575 million. So simply looking at the quantitative side of things without considering the present value of the money you earn over time, the "value" of your career is estimated to be $2.575 million. Seems simple enough, right? Not so fast!

Let's use a different approach that will allow you to more completely explore both the quantitative *and* qualitative aspects of this scenario so you can best calculate your total career value.

As said, total career value comprises two distinct yet inter-related components, the *Career Financial Value* (quantitative) and *Career Qualitative Value.*

The following Career Asset Management formula allows you to estimate *current* total career value as a baseline for any career development work you may want to undertake.

Career Financial Value (CFV) =

(Present value of Wages + PV of Benefits) - (PV of Employment Costs)

- » Wages= salary + bonuses + reimbursements

- » Benefits= employee benefits (pension, health and welfare, vacation time, etc.) + government benefits (Social Security, Medicare, etc.)

- » Employment costs= employment taxes + transportation + tools and supplies + education and training + business-related costs (clothing, meals, entertainment, etc.) + child care/family care + networking

---

The CFV formula applies to discrete (defined, fixed) and absolute (estimated) total working time periods. It measures the quantitative values of the career asset in financial terms and impacts the financial side of career satisfaction. Wages and employee benefits have a positive value or correlation to satisfaction because as these increase, so does career satisfaction up to a certain limit (diminishing returns).

Employment costs have a negative value because they decrease wages or take-home pay.

QUALITATIVE FACTORS

Assessing the qualitative factors related to career can be very subjective. What is important to one person may not matter in the least to another. Some may place a high value on working in a place surrounded by close friends while others prefer not to mix business and non-business relationships. There are numerous qualitative factors that can contribute to helping you quantify your total career value even though those factors are difficult to assign a dollar amount to.

For example, there is a value in your career knowledge. You worked hard for years becoming a subject matter expert in your field. People come to you for answers or for your perspective about a situation or problem based on your industry, institutional or technical knowledge. Keep in mind, however, knowledge value declines over time as relevant job skills change. This decline is greatest and most evident in high tech careers where technology changes at such a drastic pace that relevant job skills from just a few years ago have reduced value today. Individuals may find satisfaction in knowing they are on the cutting edge of their industry but experience dissatisfaction when they either reenter the work force after an extended period or have been remiss in maintaining their relevant skills.

We spend a third of our time at work—for many it might even be more than that! Your work connections represent the interpersonal relationships that are developed over time through things like shared experiences, common goals, networking, and simply the outcome of spending at least one-third of your lives together. The need to be connected to others is a basic human need and there is a value in feeling and being connected to others. When we change something about the way we work (our hours, location, role or even company), it impacts our connections and the real or perceived value of those connections.

Another qualitative value comes in the form of experience, maturity, and wisdom. The loss of this value at retirement (or other significant work change) can be reduced if the person replaces working with pursuits that they find intellectually inspiring and challenging but may not necessarily align with the person's historical work experiences.

The job satisfaction qualitative value measures the intrinsic rewards of a job, such as feelings of control over work and your sense of accomplishment. Also included is satisfaction with manager and co-worker relationships and feelings of appreciation and respect from the organization. Those who are self-employed often derive job satisfaction from opportunity and achievement as a substitute for organizational respect and appreciation.

The family qualitative value takes into account the connection of career with an individual's family life. Achieving a comfortable work+life fit and assessing how well work fits into the demands of family life is one of the determinants of job satisfaction.

The comparative importance of each career qualitative value varies. Some individuals derive more job satisfaction from relationships with co-workers, whereas others may value work independence and achievement as more important values.

One tool for exploring and measuring career qualitative values is a subjective wellbeing (SWB) questionnaire. SWB questionnaires have been extensively researched and effectively used in psychology and management disciplines to measure factors related to overall life satisfaction.

An easy to find example of a subjective wellbeing assessment can be found in Tom Rath and Jim Harter's book *Wellbeing: The Five Essential Elements*. This book provides an excellent resource and measurement tool for career, social, financial, physical, and community wellbeing that can be tracked over time. Of the five elements, career wellbeing is identified as the one having the greatest impact on overall wellbeing. (Harter, Rath, 2010)

Total Career Value (TCV) =

CFV (Quantitative) + Career Qualitative Value

Use of the total career value formula to measure performance of your career asset should be both relative in comparison to similar job descriptions and absolute as to achievement of individual career, personal, and family goals.

UNDERSTANDING YOUR CAREER ASSET LIFECYCLE

Just as in all other aspects of life, your career goes through a natural evolutionary lifecycle. While the phases appear on the surface to be directly related to age/life phases, they differ somewhat in the opportunity they present for building financial awareness and personal habits and actions around money. We'll take a closer look at each of the phases and draw some distinctions among them. Recognizing where you currently are in your own career lifecycle will assist you in developing, managing and optimizing your career asset.

- *Pre-career phase*
- *Early career phase*
- *Mid-career phase*
- *Late-career phase*
- *Encore career phase*

PRE-CAREER

Long before you ever think about your first after-school job, your attitudes about money are formed. You develop what financial advisor, Rick Kahler, describes as "money scripts," and they continue to influence, guide and perhaps even control your thoughts, actions and reactions to money throughout your life. Even before you're aware of their existence, they are having an impact on your choices and decisions.

Recognizing where you currently are in your own career lifecycle will assist you in developing, managing and optimizing your career asset.

Try to think back to your earliest experience with money. Where were you? Who else was present? What was the situation? How did it make you feel? One career makeover client related a story from her childhood that serves as an excellent example of how money scripts are formed and continue to operate behind the scenes:

I was about five years old and I walked into my parents' bedroom and my mother was there sitting on the bed with what seemed like a mountain of papers spread all around her. She looked, at least to me, like she was very upset. She picked up one stack of papers, consulted a little book in a plastic cover, and slammed the stack down on the bed with a heavy sigh.

"How are we going to do it?" she said. "I can't make this work. We'll never have enough money for all of this."

I remember becoming frightened and not feeling like I could share that concern with anyone. In those days, children weren't supposed to know about the family business and we certainly were not allowed to openly discuss it, even amongst ourselves. The fact that this scene was not a one-time occurrence further instilled fear, uncertainty and doubt. Every day I thought I'd come home from school to some disastrous news like our home was gone or we had to sell the car to buy food. In the extreme I even envisioned my parents having to send me back to the orphanage from where they had rescued me just a few years prior. In my limited life experience, that's what people did when they ran out of money.

Throughout my life, the idea of "we'll never have enough" continued to be driving force behind my actions and decisions. As soon as I could, I got to work and I haven't ever stopped. The idea of someday retiring is almost foreign to me as I can't accept that I'll have enough to be able to retire without worry. I started working when I was eleven, delivering a weekly sales slick door-to-door for $50 a month. I gave $10 a month to my parents—the rule in our house was if you were old enough to work, you were old enough to contribute. I put $2 in my weekly church envelope and the remaining money I squirrelled away in a tin box under my bed until my mom took me to the bank to get my first passbook savings account.

I loved feeling like I had money in my pocket. When it was cold and rainy and I didn't want to hand out those silly papers that no one ever seemed to read (I'd find previous issues still rolled up on the porches of many of assigned addressed from one week to the next), I'd remember how it felt to open that envelope every month and make my proud trip to the bank with my little green passbook.

As I grew older, "we'll never have enough" guided my decisions about what kind of car I could afford,

As I grew older, "we'll never have enough" guided my decisions.

61

where I would live, what I would buy (or not buy) at the grocery store. I taught myself to sew to save money on clothing costs. It didn't seem to matter how much earned, I couldn't shake the belief that it somehow wouldn't be enough.

This client's deeply held script continued to be a theme as we worked on her career makeover. After nearly three decades of a successful career in increasingly high pressure roles, she wanted to add some flexibility to her life. Fear of "never having enough" or running out of her reserve was a major consideration in her career makeover and led her to more than one sleepless night.

Today, that client is a successful self-employed consultant, bringing her strengths and talents to her clients across the country. She has achieved balance and the work+life fit she sought. That's not to say her "never enough" script has disappeared. But today she uses it as a catalyst for action; as a driver and motivator. During our semi-annual reviews, we know that emphasizing how her money is working for her to help her enjoy the life she now leads is an important outcome for her sense of wellbeing.

To learn more about money scripts and how they play out though life, I suggest you read *The Financial Wisdom of Ebenezer Scrooge*, (T. Klontz, R. Kahler, & B. Klontz, 2006)

Although money scripts are often formed early in life, new ones are formed based on our experiences throughout life. That's why the pre-career phase can be so influential of the rest of the career lifecycle.

The pre-career phase is the formative phase and includes your earliest experiences with work, including the development of attitudes and beliefs about the value of work. This is a phase of exploration, of developing basic job skills that will ultimately make you a more marketable employee. This is the time of life when you learn to foster the success habit of lifelong learning. We'll talk more about success habits a bit later.

It's also in this phase that our work ethic is developed. Our attitudes about work, the value of what we contribute, commitment, loyalty, relationships, control, and many more are formed and more deeply entrenched every day.

Suffice it to say, this is the critical formative phase that sets the stage for developing and ultimately managing and optimizing your career asset.

All we really have to do is observe a five-year-old at play to see how learning takes place and what charges them up (besides sugar, of course!). The wonderment of discovery, the process of learning, and picking and choosing those things that are of interest, the investment of time into those things that solicit that wonderful, unabashed happiness and focused attention—these are hallmarks of a process that continues throughout your life and career. These are the times when talents are born and begin their march toward the eventual strengths that enable a developed career.

We've all heard battle stories about children who pursued academic degrees based on what their parents wanted them to do rather than what they felt drawn to pursue. Sometimes that path works out, but all too often it results in an unsatisfactory work+life fit, unsatisfying work, or skill/talent/passion misalignment. As demonstrated in earlier chapters, these negative outcomes have the effect of lowering your career qualitative value and limiting the full potential of your career asset.

The pre-career phase represents a time for experiences such as high school and college internships. The opportunities provide a test-drive of sorts and allow the young person the chance try on different types of work to better assess what feels like a good fit.

This phase represents an excellent opportunity for adults to help the young person develop good habits around their money. Setting up a savings account or using a tool such as The Money Savvy Pig piggy bank helps children learn money management principals and develop healthy money habits from an early age. The Money Savvy Pig (also available in a Cow version for those who prefer the bovine alternative), provides four slots for young people to divvy up their earnings: saving, spending, donating, and investing.

Another strategy some parents use with their young adult children is to charge rent for living at home once the child is working. I have a client whose son moved back home after completing his undergraduate degree but before he found gainful employment. Within a few months he landed a job. Recognizing it would take some time to build financial reserves in order to move out on his own, my client began charging her son rent at an amount that was similar to what he would be paying when he moved out on his own. Six months later when my client's son was prepared and financially able to self-sustain, she returned the rent she had collected from him to fund his security deposit or to buy furniture. During the six months, he had adjusted to post-college life, formulated a workable budget, and was ready to be fiscally responsible on his own.

Healthy money habits often formed early in life and reinforced during the pre-career phase can last throughout life and contribute to sustained financial wellbeing.

EARLY CAREER

The early-career phase—typically the time of life from post-college to mid-30s,—involves initial work exposure and experience in a chosen or related field after completing college or technical training. Taking the time to properly prepare, conduct, follow-up, negotiate and accept a job offer can be time consuming and challenging in the face of early career enthusiasm and desire for "gainful employment."

There are lots of readily available resources to help the early career candidate on their path to employment so we won't cover those strategies and tactics here. Rather, there are a few financial implications of this phase that are particularly salient to career asset management.

First, for many, the early career phase is the person's first exposure to financial independence. It's the time when even minimal starting salaries represent a huge step up from the babysitting or paper route income generated in the pre-career phase. It's typically the first time a person is eligible to get a credit card or a loan for something other than academic-related pursuits. The attraction of a new car and a fancy apartment filled with contemporary furniture and lots of other fun toys is likely to present a clear and present danger to early career earner.

The trick is to avoid personal consumption credit (yes, that means throwing away those low-opening rate credit card offers that flood new grads' mailboxes or better yet, never getting one). A used car offers a viable alternative to the heavy debt load of a brand new car that depreciates in value as soon as it's driven off the lot. Renting an apartment or buying a house within means—meaning not buying more than truly can be afforded—will help ensure you can continue to build your personal use assets in a manner that is in keeping with your present earning.

When it comes to developing the career asset, this phase offers you the opportunity to advance skills and talents through seminars, workshops, conventions, job promotions and on-the-job experiences that expose you to a variety of job related aspects or even to different types of jobs. Young people may be asked to relocate, giving them an opportunity to quickly grow their value and experience, visibility, and exposure. Taking advantage of these early career opportunities is easier to do if not burdened by a lot of excess personal consumption debt.

If you work for a company that truly doesn't subscribe to a value of lifelong learning and continuous development, you might not want to rent your career out to that particular tenant for very long.

If you work for an employer that does not invest in your development or only offers those opportunities to its mid-career talent, you might consider putting your own money aside to help fund your ongoing learning or skills advancement. That investment will make you more marketable. If you work for a company that truly doesn't subscribe to a value of lifelong learning and continuous development, you might not want to rent your career out to that particular tenant for very long.

Early career is a perfect time to advance the healthy money habits from the pre-career phase by taking advantage of employer-sponsored retirement plans such as a 401k or 403b (non-profit) or a 457 deferred compensation plan for public employees. In this life/career phase, contribute the greatest of 5 percent of your compensation or meet the maximum match offered by the company. For example, some employers offer 50 cents on every $1 you put aside up to the first 10 percent of wages. If you're given an opportunity to start saving early, take it! It will grow your financial assets and contribute to your future wellbeing and financial peace of mind.

This table illustrates the significance of starting this process in early career.

REQUIRED SAVINGS AMOUNT TO ACCUMULATE $1,000,000 BY AGE 65

Starting Age	Monthly Savings	Annual Savings
20	$662	$7,950
30	$1,094	$13,133
40	$1,945	$23,340
50	$4,064	$48,763

4 percent annual growth; monthly compounding

MID-CAREER

This phase typically occurs during the highest financial need phase of life. This is the phase when most people begin their families and invest more in their housing than previously. You may buy a bigger house to accommodate your growing family or one in a neighborhood that offers better schools. It's a time when insurance costs are greater, and more individuals experience higher levels of financial strain than at other phases.

This is the phase when your career is truly developed and you're moving toward optimizing it to increased levels of performance and potential. You're putting more of your earnings into your company-sponsored plan or setting up a ROTH or other long-term savings plan to help fund your post-full-time employment years.

You might be feeling well liked and secure in your current role and confident that your skills have been honed to a point where you can easily market them to another employer should you decide to make a change (provided, of course, you've continued to develop your skills by properly managing your career asset). You might be considered for promotion or have been identified as "high potential talent" at your company, which gives you opportunities to take on new roles and assignments and increase your earning potential and value to the company exponentially faster than the typical three to four percent yearly merit increase. You may be awarded stock options or other retention incentives, which also contribute to your total career value both quantitatively and qualitatively.

If you've taken a more entrepreneurial path, this phase manifests in increased sales and business growth, expansion opportunities, and a consistent steady income that allows you to live within your means while still having sufficient funds left over to save, donate and invest.

LATE CAREER

Congratulations! You've been in the workforce for 20 to 30 years or more and your income is likely to be at its highest level. If you've properly developed and managed your career, you're now fully optimizing it to add the greatest value to your employer or business. You've earned your stripes with life experiences and you're often looked to as a resource for institutional knowledge. You may be mentoring some early or mid-career talent.

Things are looking pretty good overall. Then life happens. While the advantages of this phase are many, it's also the most vulnerable phase of your working life. This is a phase when it's easier to take a good thing for granted and assume the high-paying job you hold will never be at risk. It becomes easier to take your eye off improving and developing new ways to add value. It's easy to put your career on auto pilot and assume that what got you to where you are will be enough to keep you there.

Any dysfunctions around your career asset that might have been forged in earlier career phases will come home to roost in this one. If you haven't kept your skills current with ever-changing needs, if you haven't invested time and patience in networking and building your resources, or if you've lived beyond your financial means, you will be even more vulnerable.

It was addressing these issues with clients in this phase that served as the catalyst for developing Career Asset Management and led me to integrate it into my financial planning service model. As I saw more clients who were looking to retire as an escape hatch from unfulfilling work, I recognized a distressing trend among late career workers. These people were willing to unwittingly sabotage their most valuable asset. And I was confident that there were ways to show them potential alternatives to the faulty "all or nothing" premise they were relying on to make their decisions.

I also started seeing more clients who were victims of downsizing or job eliminations. I saw clients who felt they exhausted their value-add and were targets for replacement by early career hotshots who commanded lower salaries for fresher skills. The reality is the loss of late-career talent can end up costing a company more than retaining those employees, but few companies truly appreciate longer-range perspective on employee retention.

Several career makeover participants recognized they could achieve the work+life fit they were seeking by changing the employee agreement they had with their existing companies.

Several career makeover participants recognized they could achieve the work+life fit they were seeking by changing the employee agreement they had with their existing companies. Some opted for reduced hours, some were open to new roles within their companies, and some formally exited their current role and returned to their same companies on a consulting basis. Today, this allows the company the advantage of capitalizing on the knowledge and experience of a known worker while reducing their overall costs in benefits, full-time headcount, space and other factors.

While not ideal for every late-career worker, renegotiating your employment contract with your existing employer offers a creative alternative that benefits all parties.

ENCORE PHASE

A newer distinction in terms of career phases, the encore phase is characterized as that period of life from about age 55 or 60 to 10 years prior to end of life.

Eight thousand people a day—one every ten seconds—turns 60. The average life expectancy of a person today is over 80 years old. A healthy person entering retirement at age 62 might reasonably expect to be retired for 25 years or more. And today, we experience many more definitions of "retirement" than we have historically.

In 1990, the International Labour Organization identified retirement as being that phase of life when a person is "no longer economically active." I don't think that definition holds true for many today for several reasons, including increased life expectancy, quality of life factors, and a brutal economy. Now people are economi-

Now people are economically active longer with many working longer as a means to extend their career asset and as a way to remain active within their communities and areas of expertise.

cally active longer with many working longer as a means to extend their career asset and as a way to remain active within their communities and areas of expertise.

But what is significantly different is the way that people of traditional retirement age are choosing to work and remain economically active. Marc Freedman in his book, *The Big Shift—Navigating the New Stage Beyond Midlife*, explores a life phase known as the "third age"—that period of time after middle age, but before old age. It is during this life phase that, under the old strictures, many would retire to a life of relative leisure, relaxing after a long and fruitful working life. Today, however, more and more people are using the third age as a period to enter second careers, learn new skills, volunteer more, or pursue a delayed vocational dream. Freedman describes this age as a "sweet spot, a confluence rather than a reinvention," and a life phase when people bring added wisdom and insights to bear on the things that matter most to them. (Freedman, 2011)

Freedman outlines a 10-point plan for developing intentionality in what he calls the third age phase. Included in the plan are approaches for letting go of some of our long-held beliefs about aging and retirement and boldly forging new paths not based on preconceived notions of what is or should be characteristic of the age. He encourages us to consider creating new dreams with new definitions of success and perhaps indulging in a "gap year" in which we pause and reflect on the occurring transition. He explores options for retraining and reeducating, for pursuing service work such as the Peace Corps, and embarking on another career that would be a possibility in those years after traditional retirement.

The dictionary defines "encore" as meaning the demand by an audience for an additional performance. I tend to view what Freedman describes as the third age as being the encore life stage—a chance to provide an additional performance in those areas of deepest meaning, to add more value, to continue contributing through consulting or other non-traditional work assignments. I see the third age as having the potential of being nothing short of a brilliant encore.

Another advantage of the encore career phase is it allows you to continue to defer withdrawals from your pension income, 401K and or Social Security. Deferring withdraws allows those financial assets to continue to grow while the income you derived from your encore work substitutes for what would otherwise be needed as distributions from those assets to fund standard-of-living expenses. Deferring Social Security and pension income in the early years means you can take more in distributions in the later years. Pension and Social Security ensure increased income sources that you cannot outlive. For every year of deferral of Social Security between the ages of 62 and 70 (which is the maximum age of deferral), you will enjoy an increased annual Social Security benefit of around 8 percent.

HABITS OF CAREER SUSTAINABILITY
STRATEGIES TO FORTIFY YOUR CAREER ASSET

As its primary owner, it's up to you to ensure that your career asset continues to thrive at its highest value. The following three strategies, if exercised over your working life, will help ensure your career will remain viable and reward you with the benefits of increased job security and satisfaction in an ever changing world.

You may ask, "How can anyone be assured of job security today?" That is a fair question. The best way to ensure you have control over the many aspects of job security is to have skills that are continuously updated. This action will ensure that you remain relevant in an ever-changing global market and be positioned to exchange those skills in the market. This is where the three career strategies or habits come into play.

The best way to ensure you have control over the many aspects of job security is to have skills that are continuously updated.

HABIT #1—ACTIVELY ENGAGE IN LIFELONG LEARNING

The first career sustainability habit is to adopt a practice of lifelong learning. This learning can start as part of a goal to obtain a degree or certificate. That form of formal learning ends with the achievement of the sought after degree or certificate, which leads to the more important learning, namely, keeping your career skills relevant through continuing education. This can be part of maintaining your credentials by taking classes or attending required workshops. Certified public accountants, teachers, attorneys, architects, and other professionals comply with continuing education requirements to maintain their credentials.

For the same reasons those professionals require continuing education, we all should employ this strategy to maximize our career value. Ask your employer what learning opportunities exist for you to advance in your field. Your employer may be part of a trade or industry association that offers skill development or education. At the very least, subscribe to trade publications and be current on new developments in your field and industry. By staying informed, inevitable changes will not come as a surprise but represent opportunities for you to acquire the necessary skills to compete and advance.

HABIT #2—BENCHMARK YOUR CAREER ASSET

The second career sustainability habit is to periodically check the value of your career skill set (at least once every two years). You do this by benchmarking your job or skills against the market. Depending on the type of employment, you can find this information online or by using a career counselor/coach. One site that provides salary benchmarking is www.salary.com. By knowing what value your job skills represent, you can better negotiate salary and benefits. You can also identify skills you may be lacking that are limiting your highest potential value.

Benchmarking can also determine if you are currently overpaid for your responsibilities and skills. Yes, that does happen and when it does, know you are at risk. I have seen this first-hand after benchmarking a client's market value against his current compensation. He was overpaid by more than 30 percent. By the time we discovered this, there was little else to do but prepare him for a job change. At least we had more than a year to work on his next job before his management recognized they were overpaying for the skill and laid him off.

HABIT #3—NETWORK, NETWORK, NETWORK

The third career sustainability habit is networking. This is the ongoing process of communicating your skills in the market. Look at networking within your company/industry and outside. You network within your company/industry by establishing and increasing visibility for your skills and the value that you add. Join general and professional organizations within your field. You can find the most appropriate organization by going to your local library and checking out the Encyclopedia of Associations published by Gale Directory Library. A number of libraries do offer an online version of the Encyclopedia of Associations so check if available and save the trip.

Networking outside your industry is best done by joining various service and business organizations. Volunteering is one of the best ways to network and demonstrate your skills to other members of that organization, along with the reward of contributing to a worthwhile cause.

Often I hear from clients that they are just too busy to attend professional association meetings, conferences and other opportunities to network, benchmark skills, and build capability. I recognize the challenges of balancing a busy life with a highly engaged career; however, we can also use technology to assist us in the sustainable habit of networking.

At a minimum everyone in the professional job market should be using LinkedIn. LinkedIn is a no-cost (or low-cost) Internet-based solution for finding and maintaining contacts and connections with business associates and their contacts. For an excellent resource on maximizing the power of LinkedIn, be sure to read Wayne Breitbarth's book, *The Power Formula for LinkedIn Success.*

"How powerful is LinkedIn?" you may ask. LinkedIn has been directly responsible for job-seeking clients to find employment. For my self-employed, project-based worker clients it has led to new clients and projects for just the cost of their time to update and maintain their profiles. LinkedIn is growing in credibility and functionality every day and is quickly becoming the go-to source for recruiters and those interested in finding talent to satisfy a specific need.

By building discipline around these three habits, you can ensure your most valuable financial asset will evolve to its highest potential. If you don't quite feel comfortable implementing these strategies or just need some extra guidance, consider hiring resources to help you. The end of this book provides an overview of the various types of professionals available and the value they can bring to help you manage your career asset, regardless of where you are in your career lifecycle.

UNDERSTANDING THE RISKS

The shift from a manufacturing economy to a knowledge economy has impacted the value of certain types of careers. As explored earlier, in today's knowledge economy there is little need for some of the types of jobs and roles that were predominant during the manufacturing era.

Investopedia defines knowledge economy as:

"A system of consumption and production based on intellectual capital. The knowledge economy commonly makes up a large share of all economic activity in developed countries. In a knowledge economy, a significant part of a company's value may consist of intangible assets, such as the value of its workers' knowledge (intellectual capital). However, generally accepted accounting principles do not allow companies to include these assets on balance sheets."

Career and life experience have greater value in a knowledge economy than they do in a manual labor or manufacturing economy that was driven by more redundant types of skills. Those roles required the development of a skill or trade often as an apprentice or journeyman. While they required careful attention, they were not necessarily intellectual roles requiring a great deal of information and input to continuously improve. They required dedicated practice and experience.

Today we see more emphasis on talents and strengths that require less routine activities. Problem solving, analysis, information gathering and synthesizing, ideating and other more cerebral mechanisms are used. Decisions may change based on new inputs and new information increasing the demand for agility and flexibility.

These demographic, economic and role shifts, to say nothing of financial uncertainty, have led companies to be increasingly creative in their talent acquisition, retention, and development practices.

Given the economic decline of recent years and the reluctance of employers to hire permanent, full-time employees for anything less than mission-critical roles, project-based employment and other non-traditional work models are emerging as attractive alternatives to employers and job seekers alike. This shift in how work gets done also presents different options for employees who might feel that retirement is the only option to escape an unsatisfying current job or even career.

Just as capital needs to be quickly redeployed in response to new opportunities, human capital needs to be adaptable to rapid change. But few workers can easily plot out increasingly complex careers or evaluate potential improvements in their work/life fit. That's where career development professionals and financial planners can offer significant value by understanding your goals, objectively analyzing the current situation, thinking creatively about options and presenting ideas for positive change that won't damage your valuable career asset.

Another area of significant risk to your career asset is velocity, or the number and frequency of job changes and volatility or the fluctuations you experience in pay over time. In the next chapter, you'll see how these risks influence how you fund the management, development and optimization of your career asset.

FUNDING YOUR CAREER ASSET WITH THE CAREER ASSET WORKING CAPITAL FUND

The Career Asset Working Capital Fund (CAWCF) is a reserve fund separate from your emergency cash reserves that is established to help you develop, maintain and optimize your career asset. Financial planners often advise clients to maintain cash reserves of three to six months' living expenses. In funding your career asset, however, the amount of the Career Asset Working Capital Fund varies based on two risk factors: career velocity—the number of jobs changes, and volatility—income fluctuations over time.

Working capital for the career asset has three parts—funding skill set maintenance and development (lifelong learning), funding job changes and funding career sabbaticals or periods of family medical leave (FMLA). The working capital for the career asset should be viewed separately from your personal or family emergency cash reserves which should be sufficiently funded to allow for a minimum of three months of fully burdened living expenses, including mortgage/rent, utilities, food, and other day-to-day items in the event of job loss or other income-limiting event.

The costs of skill set maintenance and development would be primarily reflected as an expense on the income statement or budget. However, there should also be an amount in the working capital reserve to fund an unforeseen need to develop career skills. The appropriate amount would be determined based on the nature of the career. For example, if you're in a profession that requires ongoing continuing education to maintain certain credentials, the costs associated with those continuing education credits should become part of your fund. Similarly, you may identify the need to significantly improve skills in a certain aspect of your work in order to remain current and highly valued by your employer. Knowing how to access information and quickly adapt and integrate it into your work is a significant competitive advantage and will keep you ahead of your contemporaries.

The second part of the working capital fund financially supports job changes that come as a result of layoff, dismissal or voluntary exit from a current job or role. According to a recent study reported by Monster.com, the average number of weeks between jobs for workers under age 50 is 17 weeks. Over age 50 and the number of weeks of unemployment grows to 22. The U.S. Department of Labor, Bureau of Labor Statistics predicts the average number of job changes for a young worker today to be nine. These studies, along with our economic climate, dictate that a fund to cover the costs of changing jobs is a necessary part of any personal financial plan.

The last element of the Career Asset Working Capital Fund is the cost of a career sabbatical. Career sabbaticals are necessary for career rehabilitation and family or personal transitions and can extend from three months on up to a few years. Career sabbaticals can be used for re-education or training, for family care time off, for self-exploration or simply for a break from the stressors of work. The idea of a career sabbatical is to re-engineer your career so you can ultimately extend the useful life of your career asset. In order to do so, however, a thoughtful approach must be taken to fund the career sabbatical sufficiently as to not increase your debt, require you to begin early distributions from 401K plans or Social Security or otherwise damage your financial wellbeing.

The career sabbatical is a time of renewal and refocus of your career asset.

THE CAREER ASSET WORKING CAPITAL FUND IN PRACTICE

Mary is married and at age 33 she is a patent attorney with a large law firm. She has been with the firm since graduating from law school six years ago. Her annual compensation is $70,000 based on a weekly average work load of 50 hours. She plans to reduce her work load from 50 hours per week to around 30 as soon as she becomes pregnant with their first child. She plans to have two children and is uncertain as to her work status for the next five years as she plans on part-time employment until her children are ready for pre-school.

Her husband Mike, age 35, is a risk management director for a manufacturing company. His annual compensation is $75,000. He has been employed with this company for the past three years. Prior to this job, he was employed by a commercial lines insurance company in the underwriting department. He has a business degree in accounting and finance and just recently started an executive MBA program, which *he should complete in the next two years. His employer is paying for the education cost under a tuition reimbursement plan requiring his continued employment for five years after completion. The cost of the MBA program is $45,000.*

Both Mary and Mike have moderate career velocity. A contributing factor for velocity in Mary's case is her family, while for Mike it is risks inherent within the manufacturing industry along with constant change in his field of risk management. Mike is preparing for career change by continuing his education and preparing for advancement to higher corporate management positions.

Career volatility for the couple is considered moderate because both are employed in stable earning jobs. There is not much fluctuation in compensation with their current employment. That could change as both Mary and Mike explore new career opportunities over their late career working years.

Career asset maintenance costs would include continuing education for Mary both to maintain her law license and to keep current in her specialty. A reasonable annual budget of $3,000 to $4,000 is identified to cover these costs. Mike should budget the cost of at least one annual industry conference and look into certificate programs relevant to his specialty after completion of MBA program. Annual cost for a conference—$2,000 to $3,000.

Income: Combined annual income is $150,000. Total living expenses are $60,000. Taxes total $30,000. Annual savings including 401(k) and after-tax investments total $25,000.

- *Assets: Cash and checking is $30,000. After-tax investments are $40,000. Retirement savings are*

$100,000. Home value is $300,000. Two vehicles valued at $30,000 and personal property of $30,000.

- *Liabilities: Home mortgage of $210,000. Student loan of $10,000 for Mary and $45,000 contingent liability for Mike's MBA program. No consumer debt.*

Based on the abbreviated financial and career information, the amount of funds in the CAWCF should be around $95,000 to $100,000. This is based on the three parts that make up CAWCF. The first part of the reserve is one year's budgeted cost to maintain and develop both careers ($5,000 to $7,000). The second part is made up of a reserve for job change risk. The estimate of time between job loss and on-boarding a new job based on each of their salaries should average around seven months. An estimated $35,000 would cover seven months of current living expenses. The third part of the fund would be to support career sabbatical or Family Medical Leave Act (FMLA) decisions. The only anticipated event in this category is for pregnancy, childbirth and some time off for parenting. Since Mary and Mike have a modest standard of living relative to income, they could reasonably get by on one year of living expenses—$60,000.

INVESTMENT ALLOCATION OF THE CAWCF

What is a reasonable investment allocation for the CAWCF? Not all the funds need to be held in cash since much of the fund is based on future events and contingencies. Some cash is necessary—the amount for career maintenance and development and any contingencies less than two years. For the longer-term items, such as sabbaticals and FMLA, using fixed income and lines of credit are more appropriate. Each case needs to be considered based on the facts and circumstances.

In the example above, Mary and Mike have $30,000 of available equity in their home for a line of credit. After-tax investments of $40,000 should be invested in stable assets such as fixed income—perhaps Series I savings bonds or Treasury Inflation Protected Bonds (TIPs bonds). Their cash reserves of $30,000 would barely cover the total CAWCF needed. It may have seemed that they had an excess of liquidity in cash reserves and after-tax investments until we estimate an appropriate amount for the CAWCF.

A worthwhile consideration is using 529 and Educational IRA accounts for funding of educational pursuits as part of their career asset working capital fund. This will provide investment income tax deferral while the funds are not needed.

CAREER ASSET MANAGEMENT MODEL

As I was developing practice model theories for career asset management it occurred to me that the financial planning six-step process would be a good model from which to expand and integrate career asset management. The traditional six-step financial planning model includes:

1. Defining the scope of the relationship
2. Discovery and data gathering
3. Analyzing the current state
4. Developing the written plan
5. Creating implementation steps
6. Monitoring and reviewing

Let's look at each step in detail and in relationship to developing, managing and optimizing your career asset:

STEP #1: DEFINING THE SCOPE OF THE RELATIONSHIP.

Before engaging the services of a financial planner and career coach to work collaboratively with you on your career asset, it is important to explore what they're going to do for you as it relates to your desired outcomes. By having clarity of your desired outcomes along with what the service providers are going to do to help you achieve them, you reduce the possibility of missteps or misunderstandings that could derail your progress toward your ultimate goal.

It's helpful to understand each provider's services and fees from the onset of the relationship. It's recommended to ask how you will be billed, if charges are derived from an hourly, project or retainer rate; and what exactly the fee includes, as well as things that are out-of-scope or to be billed separately.

For example, if the career coach you are considering does not include professional résumé writing services as part of his or her scope, you may need to bring another resource to the table to complete that item.

Understanding the compensation model for your financial planner can be tricky. Here's a quick rundown so you can recognize the different models:

Fee-only financial planners receive no commission from the sale of any financial product such as insurance or investment vehicles. This eliminates the conflict of interest that might arise from recommending financial vehicles that aren't really appropriate for your particular needs or desired objectives. Many fee-only financial planners are financial life planners, meaning they create a long-term relationship, using a wider lens through which to view all aspects of your financial wellbeing over time.

Fee-based planners collect both commissions on financial products they are licensed to sell along with fees (usually based on investment assets under management—AUM). Under this arrangement you will pay your advisor a fee that is directly related to your investment portfolio—meaning the more assets you have with the firm, the more fees you pay. Under this business model, it is unlikely the planner would recommend redeploying investments for improving and developing your career as this would conflict with the planner's primary emphasis on growing the amount of investments under management. Higher AUM=more fees collected. If you reduce your AUM by, let's say, $100,000 to fund a career sabbatical, the planner's compensation would be reduced.

Some planners are paid on an hourly basis for the advice they provide on a specific financial product or to help you with a specific area of your personal finances. These are often very limited engagements with the intent of addressing specific aspects of your personal financial picture rather than taking a broader financial life planning perspective.

Be sure to ask your service provider to describe how your proposed engagement will end. Include this discussion as part of your exploratory conversation with all service providers you consider.

The last method of financial advisor/planner compensation is commission-only. Under this arrangement, your advisor is only compensated when you purchase financial products such as insurance or investments. It should come as no surprise that this compensation method is the most problematic when it comes to conflicts of interest and the ability for the advisor to be objective.

One last point on defining the engagement is to understand the process for ending the relationship(s). Everything in life has a beginning, middle and end—including professional service engagements. Be sure to ask your service provider to describe how your proposed engagement will end. Include this discussion as part of your exploratory conversation with all service providers you consider.

STEP #2: DISCOVERY AND DATA GATHERING

The discovery data gathering step is arguably the most important in that it creates the picture of your future desired state. This can be done with the financial planner and career coach together or separately. I prefer to perform the discovery/data gathering process independent of the career coach's process because we will each be viewing the same or similar information but through different lenses.

At the end of this step, we confirm and validate your goals, objectives, values, and beliefs as understood by both the financial planner and career coach. This validation increases your confidence that you are clear with your vision of your future. If we do not have validation/confirmation, we continue with the discovery and data gathering process until we are all clear and aligned around your vision and goals for your career.

In the career asset management model, the outcomes of the discovery and data gathering step is shared between the career coach and financial planner. There are, however, areas of discovery that fall specifically within the domain of the financial planner. These areas include understanding your current financial position, including your assets and liabilities, risk management (insurances), retirement and Social Security benefits, and your estate planning objectives.

Similarly, there are areas that are within the career coach's expertise, including personal assessment tools such as Myers-Briggs, Emotional Intelligence (EQ), Kolby Assessments, StrengthsFinder and Career Anchors to name a few. Each of these tools is designed to assess different things. Not all are used in every engagement and the career coach will be able to help identify those assessments most beneficial for you to take to help bring additional clarity to your career asset based on your personality, interest areas, talents and strengths, social interaction style or others. Understanding your work history, habits, work+life fit demands, skills inventory, and experience also fall within the career coach's area of discovery.

STEP #3: ANALYZING THE CURRENT STATE

After a thorough process of discovery/data gathering, the next step involves analyzing the plethora of data as a foundation for developing the action plan. The financial planner is responsible for preparing all of the relevant personal finance statements—net worth, income, time value of money calculations for various financial goals such as funding children's or grandchildren's education, major life transitions, retirement, etc. The financial planner also explores the family environment, child and or eldercare and spouse/partner's reality and expectations as those have implications on the financial picture as well as the eventual action plan.

The current-state analysis includes work realities such as your company's work+life policies, corporate culture/work styles and your history and an exploration of anticipated opportunities specifically with your current employer and generally in your industry. This portion of the analysis is typically led by the career coach.

Shared work between financial planner and career coach includes a review of your total career value (quantitative and qualitative value), opportunity for career development and worst-case scenario visioning.

Shared work between financial planner and career coach includes a review of your total career value (quantitative and qualitative value), opportunity for career development and worst-case scenario visioning.

Let's look at each of these shared items:

Total career value includes both the quantitative and qualitative value that you currently experience. In our review, we look for opportunities to improve your career value. The starting point is to analyze your compensation compared to industry and role benchmarks.

Benchmarking is of value in two ways. First, it identifies opportunities to increase current compensation if determined to be below the benchmarked value. Second, it helps to be better positioned for the somewhat rare but risky situation in which current compensation is significantly higher than benchmarked value, putting you at greater risk for downsizing, job elimination or restructuring.

Beth was being paid over $200,000 per year for a job that her career coach benchmarked at$120,000-$140,000. In our current-state analysis we found that the employer/company (a family business) expected to be acquired by a large national company. Beth was an important contributor to the success of her employer and had longtime legacy value (over ten years) that her employer needed in place through the sale and integration with the buyer/acquirer. Beth was a strategic talent in a changing environment.

Upon learning this, Beth's initial reaction was defensive and she denied she was overcompensated. The career coach provided evidence of the overcompensation and allowed time and space for Beth to process the information. Beth's image of self-worth and value was closely tied to the compensation she earned with little thought given to risk of being priced out of her job. Collaborating with the career coach, we helped Beth see the need to prepare for the eventual loss of employment once the acquisition was completed. Within 18 months of the merger acquisition, Beth was notified her job was being eliminated. But by then, she was well positioned financially and had a more clear expectation of the market value of her skill and expertise. Beth had time to prepare for the job loss proactively rather than having to react to the shock of unexpected job loss.

What is more frequent as an outcome from benchmarking is the discovery that a client is under-compensated. This situation is easier than overcompensation since there is rarely the risk of job loss when an employee is undercompensated. That is because the undercompensated employee usually has other employment opportunities that are closer to market value, along with an employer who would have to pay more (market value) to replace him or her.

While challenging and often an intimidating prospect, a well-articulated value proposition presented by the employee to the employer can begin to correct the pay disparity based on market reference data. Another opportunity is negotiated for improved work+life fit in exchange for the lower-than-benchmark compensation. It may be of greater value to the employee to trade off monetary compensation for scheduling flexibility or work that is more inspiring and less stressful.

The second area of financial planner/career coach shared work is career development. The rate of return on acquiring new skills to develop your career will often depend on how many years you have remaining to harvest returns. These returns can be both quantifiable (financial) and/or qualitative (quality of life). Collaboratively, the career coach and financial planner can help you estimate your return on investment on your career development. Let me share a couple of cases to illustrate.

The first case is an example of career development with the desired outcome to improve the financial performance (return on investment) of one's career:

> *Terry, a public school teacher with 30 years of teaching experience, considered pursuing her master's degree. Obtaining her master's degree would not change any of the qualitative values of her career, meaning her day-to-day work activities would be the same.*
>
> *Terry expected to work five more years and questioned the return on her time and financial investment of pursuing her*

master's degree. It would take her two years and $20,000 to obtain this degree. Having a master's degree would mean an increase in her compensation of $11,682 per year.

Since it would take her two years to complete her degree, she would only be receiving the additional annual compensation for three years. However, this additional compensation would increase her state pension by $6,850 per year before income taxes. Assuming a 33-percent marginal income tax rate and a 4-percent discount rate, the after-tax present value of an additional 22 years of increased pension would amount to $67,080.

Including the three years of additional compensation, her financial return is more than three and one-half times the $20,000 financial investment she made in her career. The internal rate of return of cash flows over Mary's 22 year life expectancy is more than 27 percent.

Granted, Terry has to add to the financial investment her time and effort to obtain her master's degree, but where can you find a guaranteed investment return of more than 27 percent?

The second case involves "Theresa," and the investment in and enhancement of her skill set to prepare her for a completely different career path:

Theresa had the educational background and experience in the nutrition and public health field. This led to a job in public nutrition for a county health department. Through her discovery and data-gathering process, she determined that improved work+life fit along with more opportunities to work one-on-one with clients would be more satisfying than her current type of work.

Working with her career coach, Theresa envisioned a future as a geriatrics case manager, which required more education and training along with six months of residency. Her previous experiences would benefit her in her new job search but she still needed two years' worth of career development.

The outcome of her career development would not deliver increased financial returns, as the new role actually was benchmarked at a lower value than her role with the county health department. However, Theresa was willing to invest in her career redevelopment to better align with her vision, values and work+life fit demands.

You see, career asset management it isn't always about making more money…sometimes investing in the career asset may actually mean earning less. But you may be able to earn less per year for many more years than you may have been willing or able to do in your previous role in which you earned more in exchange for your satisfaction.

At this stage of the planning process, we have defined the scope of the relationship, we've gathered data and analyzed all the puts and takes, identified opportunities for change, quantified available resources, and determined our constraints. All of this work will contribute to the action plan for your career asset.

As identified by a number of career coaches, one of the major roadblocks to a meaningful career breakthrough the stress that comes from feeling fearful.

Negotiating an employment agreement is nerve-wracking and for many it can be downright frightening. As one client told me:

> *"I was just so happy when I got my job that I would never, ever have to go through the negotiation process again. It was so intimidating and stressful. I can't imagine leaving my current employer simply because I don't want to have to go through that again."*

Regardless of the fear-generating state negotiating an employment contract can evoke, it's likely that it's not going to be a once-in-a-lifetime event. It can even be an even more frightening task when the negotiating that must take place is with your current employer. Adding to the natural stress involved in negotiating, many people experience fear of reprisal or even job loss if the request isn't well received by the employer. This fear may be strong enough to keep undercompensated or otherwise dissatisfied employees from ever raising their concerns with their employer and opting instead to either remain in a dysfunctional situation or choose the retirement escape hatch at the earliest possible date. Either of these paths erodes the career asset.

Negotiating an employment agreement is nerve-wracking and for many it can be downright frightening.

One strategy we use to help clients process fear is worst-case scenario visioning. This scenario-based process involves facing our fears—both real and imagined. A variety of scenarios are presented that represent the worst thing that could happen for each of the possible actions we take when managing the career asset:

Joe was a very talented research scientist. He was so good, in fact, that his employer promoted him to managing a team of research scientists. His typical workday consisted of attending management meetings, individual team member meetings and reviewing the work of the research team. His passion, however, was in research and he was very good at it. Because of all the meetings he had to attend, he had little time to actually conduct research. The long hours were taking toll on his family life. He was afraid to speak directly to his immediate supervisor about his increasing dissatisfaction as he felt he'd be putting his job at risk. It was clear that his biggest fear was the fear of losing his job.

Effectively, worst-case scenario planning is like helping a young child who is afraid of what's in the dark closet—we go into the closet and turn on the light.

So this fear is what we used in our worst-case scenario visioning session. We actually envisioned Joe having a conversation with his employer that ended in his termination. We mapped out what his life would look like when he was no longer employed with his current employer. What would he do to pay his bills? How long would his financial resources cover his bills? And who would hire him?

As we went through this visioning process, Joe himself started to see that there was little chance he would lose his job and if he did, he possessed sufficient marketable skills to offer to another employer.

Effectively, worst-case scenario planning is like helping a young child who is afraid of what's in the dark closet—we go into the closet and turn on the light. The monsters feared to be in the dark closet were really only shadows.

STEP #4: DEVELOPING AN ACTION PLAN, INCLUDING YOUR CAREER ENGAGEMENT STANDARDS

This step involves articulating your career vision statement, objectives and timelines and committing them to writing. It is the culmination of the previous steps that provides you with the roadmap you will follow in implementing your plan. The level of detail can vary depending on what is necessary for clarity. For some clients brief statements are sufficient. I have seen great detail and explanation used in order for the client to feel ready to move toward implementation. The financial planner and career coach provide input to the action plan, but it really is incumbent on the client to create the physical document that will serve as his/her roadmap going forward.

It is important to include career engagement standards in formulating the career action plan.

Regardless of the detail included, it is important to include career engagement standards in formulating the career action plan. Career engagement standards allow you to become crystal clear on those things you feel are vital for your work environment and structure. By writing down your engagement standards, they become anchoring points and serve to reinforce and validate any changes you may consider in your career asset. Included in your engagement standards are things like:

- *The types of work you want and should being doing to deliver your highest value*

- *A description of how you go about doing that work and with whom you work best. Do you like to work alone or as part of a team? Do you prefer "thinking" work or "doing" work?*

- *The physical environment in which you prefer to work. Do you prefer to work in a lab with little contact with others? Do you like to be in an open space environment where you can "catch" the excitement of co-workers as they converse and go about their own work? Do you like quiet spaces or open, noisy ones? Do you feel you have to have an office with a door or is a cube acceptable?*

- *The types of tasks that drain you of energy and those that inspire you and motivate you*

- *The leadership style under which you feel you can thrive. Do you work best with direct supervision and a lot of contact with your immediate supervisor? Do you prefer to work more autonomously with less interaction?*

Your engagement standards should be clear and in writing. Working collaboratively with your career coach, you should be able to identify and articulate your standards and match them with the ideal work, physical environment and team.

That's not to say that every aspect of your engagement standards will be met by your job. You'll need to determine those items that you absolutely must have and which ones are considered nice to have but not critical. I would suggest the nice-to-have but critical ones not be included in your written engagement standard as that will become the litmus test against which you evaluate alignment between what you must have to build your career asset and what the job at hand or under review actually offers.

Engagement standards can change over time so it's recommended to review them at least every few years for relevancy and to ensure the things you felt important in your mid-career phase are still important to you in your late-career phase.

Your written career engagement standards include your career objectives and vision as well as the constraints you face in achieving that vision. Constraints are any factors that could impede your progress toward your objectives, including real or perceived financial constraints.

Your career coach and financial planner will help you identify potential constraints based on your current situation and your engagement standards.

For example, your current education/training skill set may be limiting your ability to experience your ideal career. You may need to consider returning for additional education, certifications or credentialing that will enable you to progress toward your goal.

Another potential constraint is your engagement standard related to work+life fit. This could include considerations such as your available working hours, availability for travel, family issues and the like.

For the past five years Peter has held a mid-level management position at a Fortune 500 company. As his work responsibilities grew so did the demands on his non-work time. Peter was spending a couple of hours a night reviewing emails that he couldn't keep up with during his customary 10-hour workday. He began traveling more frequently for business and for longer periods of time, which often interfered with his weekend plans. And he was participating in conference calls with colleagues and customers around the world, sometimes in the middle of the night.

When Peter joined the company five years earlier he had far fewer demands and expectations on his non-work time. Now, his children were 10 and 12 years old and involved in a wide array of extracurricular activities. His wife worked out of the home in the evenings, so dinner, homework, and bedtime routines often fell to Peter to satisfy.

The increasing demands of Peter's upward career progress compromised his ability to be fully present for his children in the way he and his wife agreed was necessary in this life phase. In effect, Peter's lack of availability for after-work work, late-night phone calls, and weekend travel was a constraint.

Time horizons or the time between significant life transitions can also be a constraint. These transitions include specific events such as children leaving for college, graduation, significant anniversaries along with transitions that lack time specificity such as a parent's end-of-life and the inevitable but unknown time for family medical leave.

And there are financial constraints. By this stage of the planning process we should have clearly identified the estimated costs associated with funding a career transition of any sort—that might be a job/career change, re-education, career sabbatical or other tactic. The cost of funding a career transition should be viewed as a capital investment similar to remodeling or rehabbing a rental property.

As mentioned under the worst-case scenario visioning process, financial fear can paralyze any meaningful progress. When considering financial constraints it is imperative to separate and isolate fear from real financial limitations.

Your written engagement standards are useful in myriad ways. You can use them to match against your real world or desired work situation. When benchmarking, you can use your engagement standards to increase or decrease the market value of a certain role based on your constraints.

When considering financial constraints it is imperative to separate and isolate fear from real financial limitations.

One of our self-employed career makeover clients who left a comfortable long-time role with a large company to become a consultant with more control over the type of work she does routinely incorporates elements of her engagement standards into her statements-of-work for her clients.

"I let them know right up front that the majority of my work is done off-site, but that I am available for conference calls during regular business hours," she told us during one of our monitor and review meetings. "Not once did one of my clients

tell me that arrangement wouldn't work for them, but if I didn't have it included in my statement of work, they might easily conclude that I would work wherever THEY wanted me to rather than where I wanted me to."

Your engagement standards, along with your career objectives and constraints, become part of your action plan. Details about the steps to take to achieve your stated objectives, the associated timelines, and financial or other considerations are mapped to the plan. Some plans call for interim steps to be taken on the path toward maximizing your career asset. In that case, the interim steps are also identified and assigned a timeline.

STEP #5: IMPLEMENTATION

Your comprehensive career asset management plan is now in place. Implementation timelines can vary greatly depending on the number of issues and overall complexity of your action plan. In the case where additional education/training is needed, implementation can take years whereas if the primary career issue is work+life fit, a renegotiation conversation with your employer could be completed in a much shorter timeframe.

Part of the implementation includes aligning your financial resources to develop, manage, and optimize your career asset. You will rely on your Career Asset Management Working Capital Fund to support your career plan implementation.

Probably the most important thing to keep in mind regarding the implementation phase is that this is a dynamic process, and you could find a high degree of variance between what you expect and what you actually discover when implementing your plan.

Your plan is your roadmap but just be cautious about missing the scenery along the way! That is, don't lose sight of your end-game, but while you're working toward it, be prepared to encounter new and potentially exciting opportunities or ideas that weren't part of your original plan. Be flexible, open, and willing to see opportunities with a different lens. But also remain consistent with the engagement standards you identified.

Don't lose sight of your end-game, but while you're working toward it, be prepared to encounter new and potentially exciting opportunities or ideas that weren't part of your original plan.

During the implementation step, your financial planner is helping you deal with quantitative issues such as tax considerations and employee benefit considerations for new opportunities. He or she will also monitor your Career Asset Management Working Capital Fund to ensure it continues to support your career asset management plan. Your career coach will work with you on accountability and help keep you on task with your plan. The coach will provide feedback and may offer guidance on interviewing skills development or scenario practice sessions.

Unfortunately, no amount of support or coaching can make your plan happen—only you have the power to do that. The implementation of your Career Asset Management plan is driven by you and supported by your planner and coach.

STEP #6: MONITOR AND REVIEW

During and after implementation of your career asset management plan, your work on your career asset continues. We call this ongoing work the monitor and review phase. This phase includes periodic benchmarking of your compensation (at least every couple years), optimizing employee benefit opportunities (annual review) and overall review of the qualitative values of your career. Additionally you must continuously practice the three habits of career sustainability—lifelong learning, benchmarking, and networking.

As part of your annual career asset management review, you'll evaluate your action plan and discuss with your planner how your job aligns with your employer's strategic and tactical goals. Over time companies' goals evolve, and strategies that support those goals change along with specific tactics and actions. You need to be clear on how your work aligns with your employer's goals even if you're in the middle of transitioning to a new role or career. The more valuable your contribution to your employer's success the more secure your employment and your ability to work within your engagement standards.

Once you've dedicated the time it takes to view your career as an asset, it's time to celebrate your accomplishment.

I like to think there is a seventh step in this process and I call it Celebrate You! Once you've dedicated the time it takes to view your career as an asset and take the necessary steps to ensure it is properly developed, managed, and optimized like other assets in your portfolio, it's time to celebrate your accomplishment.

That accomplishment might be as simple as opting to work fewer hours with your current employer rather than retiring. It might be as extreme as preparing for and entering an entirely new career path—it's never too late to do so with proper planning.

Congratulations on managing, developing, and optimizing your career. It is an investment that will yield many returns.

SUPPORTING YOU ON YOUR WAY

It's important to remember, you're not in this process alone. There are numerous resources available to help you navigate as you develop, manage, and optimize your career asset. Included among them are:

- *Financial advisors*
- *Career coaches*
- *Career counselors*
- *Professional résumé writers*

YOUR FINANCIAL ADVISOR

Over time, the traditional financial plan has evolved to include in-depth personal data gathering. Professional-standard portfolio management now includes very specific research and allocation among stocks, bonds, real estate, and a variety of vehicles that invest in them. In addition to offering the full range of financial planning strategies and tactics, a growing number of sophisticated and holistic financial life planners have incorporated Career Asset Management into their planning practices. Those typically fee-only financial advisors (meaning they charge a fee for service rather than earning their money off the commission from selling you financial products) can contribute significant value when working with you to manage, develop, and optimize your career asset by:

- *Increasing your potential income*
- *Connecting you with career coaches and other resources*
- *Improving your work+life fit and quality-of-life issues; and*
- *Helping you extend the lifecycle of your career asset*

If you don't have a financial planner yet and you're interested in finding one, there are a few important considerations to keep in mind when researching and interviewing these professionals:

- *The planner's credentials. There are many, many designations and credentials in the personal financial planning industry. Lots of fancy letters after a person's name can instill a higher degree of confidence, but if you're serious about wanting the most recognized designation of comprehensive and broad financial planning, look for a Certified Financial Planning® professional (CFP).*

- *Compensation models. As discussed previously, there are numerous compensation models that various types of financial planners use. Some derive their income from commissions earned by selling you financial products. Others charge hourly or some other fee structure. For those who have retainers or annual fees, the financial portions of Career Asset Management are typically included in the fees. It's important to understand exactly how your financial advisor is compensated—it will influence the type of relationship you have with him or her and it will indicate where the emphasis will be on helping you plan for your financial well-being.*

The National Association of Personal Financial Advisors (NAPFA) offers a free publication called "Pursuit of a Financial Advisor Field Guide." It's full of helpful thoughts, ideas, and questions to ask your prospective financial planner. Their website also offers a search engine for finding a fee-only financial advisor.

At one time the location of a financial planner was more important to clients than it appears to be in today's technologically advanced environment. Web tools like Skype enable a financial planner and client to meet virtually regardless of physical locations. We have clients all over the country and we are able to stay connected anytime there's reliable Internet service.

CAREER COACHES AND COUNSELORS

The difference between career coaches and counselors is that counselors tend to be more tactical in providing job search assistance such as providing résumé writing and interviewing techniques. Coaches use a more strategic approach in working with clients that includes identifying attitudes, beliefs, and behaviors that keep them from achieving their potential.

Stay away from potential coaches/counselors who prey on individuals desperate for employment by offering veiled guarantees of high-paying jobs in exchange for fees starting at $5,000 or more. Outplacement service organizations, (firms that provide employers job placement services for their terminated employees) generally are not good resources as they represent employers' interests. I have found that the greatest benefit of outplacement services is for the employers —mitigating the risk of an unfair termination case being brought against them. While these services can be useful for the unemployed, they should not be confused with career coaching services.

"Career management" firms or "job finding services" should be avoided. While they might present lots of data indicating success rates with helping their clients find jobs, their claims have proven to be at best inflated and at worse, downright lies.

In 2003 the Illinois Attorney General filed a complaint against a firm that had promoted themselves as being job career specialists. This firm was also brought to task in several other states. They targeted primarily middle- and upper-management job seekers, charging them between $3500 and $12,500 for often the same or similar services available online for free. The biggest deception was their representation that their services included access to a non-existent "secret" job market.

Bottom line: don't trust anyone who says they can get you a job if you pay them a fee up front. Reputable head hunters are paid by the prospective employers, not the job seekers.

Bottom line: don't trust anyone who says they can get you a job if you pay them a fee up front.

When it comes to working with a career coach or counselor, a master's or Ph.D. in behavioral sciences such as counseling and psychology with additional training in coaching is desirable. A background in human resource management with specific training in coaching and counseling is also ideal. One well-respected certification, National Certified Counselors (NCC), is conferred by the National Board for Certified Counselors. Leading outplacement companies, such as Lee Hecht Harrison, Right Management and Hewitt Associates, may refer you to individual career coaches with whom they subcontract. Other sources include ExecuNet, Career Masters International, the National Career Development Association and the Association of Career Professionals International.

With no universally recognized designation or qualification required, virtually anyone can set up business as a career coach. This makes conducting due diligence an imperative when evaluating your selection. Verify any consumer complaints filed against the candidate and check out their references. These should include references from both clients and other third-party professionals. Ask references about services used, level of satisfaction and outcome.

Look for services that include use of assessment tools and other instruments. A service review will also help you determine if your prospective provider is a coach or counselor. If services are provided on a flat fee retainer basis, be sure to identify the length of time of the engagement and who will provide the services.

PROFESSIONAL RÉSUMÉ WRITERS

Please note the first word of this section is "professional." Do not entrust this important career asset tool to an amateur. Professional résumé writers understand what goes into the process of presenting your career highlights and accomplishments in a way that is consumable by prospective employers and sophisticated applicant tracking systems (ATS) that are designed to defeat the unwary candidate.

According to Mary Jo King, a veteran pro, the primary goal of ATS is to reduce the quantity of applications that make it through the system, thereby reducing the number of candidates to a manageable level.

These systems are finicky about formatting and commonly use things like bullets, certain fonts, line positions, and section headings that could keep your résumé from ever getting to the next digital step.

According to the National Résumé Writers Association, 70 percent of uploaded résumés don't even get parsed into the system, meaning they don't even get seen. The remaining few get scored and ranked based on key word matches, so it's important to understand how key words work.

Once your résumé reaches human hands, you have only seconds to sufficiently impress the reader before being sorted into a "Yes" or "No" interview category. Important information has to *pop*, because your documents will rarely receive a full and thorough reading.

CONCLUSION

The Road to Hana is one of the most widely sought after experiences for visitors to the island of Maui. Guidebooks tout the 68-mile stretch of winding road as one of the earth's most beautiful drives. The destination is, as the name implies, Hana, a small town at the end of highway. Travelers eagerly rent jeeps and gear up for a full day's excursion to Hana and set off with as much haste as the sometimes harrowing road allows. But, the Road to Hana isn't about getting to Hana—there isn't much there when you finally do arrive. The Road to Hana is about the experience of the drive. It's about pulling off the road and exploring hidden waterfalls and spending time on secluded beaches. It's about sampling locally grown goods sold at roadside stalls. It's about yielding to traffic coming in the opposite direction in a throwback to more civil days. In short, it's the journey, not the destination that makes this trip so remarkable.

It's the journey, not the destination that makes this trip so remarkable.

I contend the road we take in developing, managing, and optimizing our careers to make them a vital asset is another remarkable journey. Along the way, we experience bumps, maybe even a flat tire or two. We might occasionally overheat and feel like we blew an engine. But then we regroup, remember what's important, recall that all of life is a journey, and move on.

Viewing your career like an asset on par with your other investments shifts the paradigm away from viewing your career as a binary; on/ off thing and toward appreciating it as an engine that fuels your own personal Road to Hana.

Enjoy the ride, take in the scenery, and learn from your experience. Manage, develop, and optimize your career asset and it will continue to take you on wonderful, exciting and beneficial adventures. Happy trails!

REFERENCE MATERIALS TO HELP YOU ENJOY THE JOURNEY

Freedman, Marc. *The Big Shift: Navigating the New Stage Beyond Midlife*. New York, N.Y.: PublicAffairs, 2011.

...Freedman uses compelling personal stories to help readers in varying stages of life and career transition create their own positive paths to fulfilling and rewarding work and lifestyle choices.

Moon, Janine. *Career Ownership: Creating 'Job Security' in Any Economy*. Parker & Shelby Press, 2010.

...Moon's unique approach to career development, which applies to readers at any stage of their professional careers, provides valuable instruction on how to partner with employers in order to create mutually satisfying, beneficial and lasting results.

Kahler, Rick, CFP, Brad Klontz, Psy.D, and Ted Klontz, Ph.D.
The Financial Wisdom of Ebenezer Scrooge: 5 Principles to Transform Your Relationship with Money. Deerfield Beach: Health Communications, Inc., 2006.

… The authors use the analogy of Ebenezer Scrooge's transformation from an angry miser to a kind and generous man to present a new way of thinking about how we think, view and act around our personal finances.

Yost, Cali Williams. *Work + Life: Finding the Fit that's Right for You.* Toronto: Penguin Publishing Group, 2004.

… Yost dispels the popular and oftentimes problematic theory that work is an end-all, be-all proposition, and provides readers with some tools to change personal and work-related realities to best fit a healthy balance for each individual.

Bridges, William, Ph.D. *Transitions: Making Sense of Life's Changes.* Cambridge: Da Capo Press, 2004.

…Bridges steps readers through three difficult stages of major life transitions (The Ending, The Neutral Zone and The Beginning) with an insightful roadmap for navigating change, and an especially helpful guide to readers at career crossroads.

Whitehead, Bert, M.B.A., J.D. *Facing Financial Dysfunction: Why Smart People do Stupid Things with Money!* Concord: Infinity Publishing, 2002

… Whitehead suggests ways to identify and treat the symptoms of financial dysfunction, taking a simple approach to helping readers review their

belief systems, resultant actions and probable outcomes in a way that helps them find healthy ways to manage finances.

Alboher, Marci. *The Encore Career Handbook: How to Make a Living and a Difference in the Second Half of Life.* New York: Workman Publishing Co., 2012.

...Designed for those considering retirement or transition into a new career this practical guide explains how you can earn a living and continue making a difference in the second half of life, and provides valuable pros and cons of many aspects around planning the transition.

Milevsky, Moshe A., Ph.D. *Are You a Stock or a Bond? Identify Your Own Human Capital for a Secure Financial Future.* Upper Saddle River: Pearson Education, Inc., 2012.

...Milevsky helps readers understand the importance of human capital as one of the most important assets in a typical person's "portfolio," and provides practical solutions on how to balance critical assets in order to achieve financial security.

Anthony, Mitch. *The New Retirementality: Planning Your Life and Living Your Dreams...at Any Age You Want.* Hoboken: Wiley, 2012.

...Anthony asks readers to recognize that today's major life and work choices are affected by realities that are vastly different from generations' past: to succeed, you need a new attitude, both means and meaning, and the investment in something he coins "return on life."

Pollan, Stephen and Mark Levine. *Second Acts: Creating the Life You Really Want, Building the Career You Truly Desire.* New York: William Morrow Paperbacks/Harper Collins, 2003.

...Pollan and Levine help readers—especially those approaching the "second act" of life—develop a dynamic "script" to help them translate their dreams into life goals, and then offer guidance on how to recognize and overcome any obstacles in order to turn those goals into realities.

Rath, Tom, and James Harder, Ph.D. *Wellbeing: The Five Essential Elements.* Washington, D.C.: Gallup Press, 2010.

...Taking a holistic view of what influences a state of wellbeing over the course of a lifetime, the authors explain how five key elements (career, social, financial, physical and community) interact to shape our lives and contribute to what makes life worthwhile.

Breitbarth, Wayne. *The Power Formula for LinkedIn Success: Kickstart Your Business, Brand, and Job Search (Second Edition —Entirely Revised).* Austin: Greenleaf Book Group Press, 2013.

...Readers learn how to tap into a powerful business tool in order to create a dynamic and engaging presence that defines and reinforces their brand, uncover critical information about employers, competitors and customers, and find new opportunities for professional growth and development.

ABOUT MICHAEL HAUBRICH, CFP®

Michael Haubrich is known throughout the financial planning industry for creatively blending traditional financial planning with contemporary thinking and tools to meet the work and life realities of today's clients. Since starting Financial Service Group in 1983, Mike has been a relationship-focused industry innovator who is passionate about his responsibility to his clients and to always putting their needs first, free from the conflicts of interest that often come when commissions for the sale of financial products are collected. Mike is proud to lead Financial Service Group and its fee-only business model.

Mike has served in the financial planning industry since 1979. The founder and president of Financial Service Group, Mike is an Investment Advisor Representative with the Securities & Exchange Commission (SEC) and has been a Certified Financial Planner™ practitioner since 1986. Mike graduated with honors from University of Wisconsin-Parkside and the College for Financial Planning.

In 2006, he introduced Career Asset Management™ (CAM) to the financial planning and career counseling professions. As a thought leader on this topic, he has been a frequent speaker at various industry events. Described as "game changing" by industry experts, CAM has also been featured in news articles and has become an adopted topic for many financial planners and career counselors throughout the country.

Mike's viewpoints have appeared in *The Wall Street Journal, Chicago Tribune, Forbes, Yahoo Hot Jobs, The Journal of Financial Planning, Investment News,* and other major industry trade publications. He also contributes to the "To Your Wealth" column published monthly in the *Racine Journal Times*.

Mike is past president of the Greater Milwaukee chapter of International Association for Financial Planning, currently the Financial Planning Association of Southern Wisconsin. He is a member of the National Association of Personal Financial Advisors (NAPFA) and past president of the Racine Kenosha Estate Planning Council. Active in the community, Michael serves on the University of Wisconsin-Parkside Foundation, Lakeside Curative Services, and Hospice Alliance boards.

ABOUT TAMI WITT

In 2008, just as the United States began experiencing the impact of the largest financial disaster since the Great Depression, Tami Witt made the bold decision to launch Asset Communication. Determined to help organizations maximize their increasingly limited resources, she embarked on an extraordinary journey working with clients of all sizes who struggled with similar issues: inadequate communication, declining employee engagement, and lacking change management processes. Applying communication expertise developed over 25 years, Tami now has offices in southeast Wisconsin and metro-Phoenix, Arizona and creates and executes strategic communication and change plans with local, national and global businesses in diverse industries including financial planning, manufacturing, consumer products, higher education, agriculture, and professional services. She is on the board of Careers Industries, serving the needs of persons with disabilities in southeast Wisconsin. You can learn more about Tami's experience and background at www.linkedin.com/in/tamiwitt

CPSIA information can be obtained at www.ICGtesting.com
Printed in the USA
BVOW09s1010131114

374977BV00028B/603/P